COLLABO

EFFEC

COLLABORATING FOR EFFECTIVENESS

Empowering schools to be inclusive

Jennifer Evans
Ingrid Lunt
Klaus Wedell
Alan Dyson

OPEN UNIVERSITY PRESS
Buckingham · Philadelphia

Open University Press
Celtic Court
22 Ballmoor
Buckingham
MK18 1XW

email: enquiries@openup.co.uk
world wide web: http://www.openup.co.uk

and
325 Chestnut Street
Philadelphia, PA 19106, USA

First Published 1999

Copyright © Jennifer Evans, Ingrid Lunt, Klaus Wedell and
Alan Dyson, 1999

All rights reserved. Except for the quotation of short passages for the purpose of criticism and review, no part of this publication may be reproduced, stored in a retrieval system, or transmitted, in any form or by any means, electronic, mechanical, photocopying, recording or otherwise, without the prior written permission of the publisher or a licence from the Copyright Licensing Agency Limited. Details of such licences (for reprographic reproduction) may be obtained from the Copyright Licensing Agency Ltd of 90 Tottenham Court Road, London, W1P 9HE.

A catalogue record of this book is available from the British Library

ISBN 0 335 20229 2 (hb)   0 335 20228 4 (pb)

Library of Congress Cataloging-in-Publication Data
Collaborating for effectiveness:empowering schools to be inclusive /
Jennifer Evans . . . [*et al.*].
   p. cm.
   Includes bibliographical references (p. 133) and index.
   ISBN 0-335-20229-2. – ISBN 0-335-20228-4 (pbk.)
   1. Inclusive education–Great Britain. 2. Learning disabled children–Education–Great Britain. 3. Inter-school cooperation–Great Britain. 4. School management and organization–Great Britain. 5. Education and state–Great Britain. I. Evans, Jennifer (Jennifer Mary).
LC1203.G7C65   1998
371.9′046–dc21   98-7256
                                                                 CIP

Typeset by Graphicraft Limited, Hong Kong
Printed in Great Britain by St Edmundsbury Press Ltd, Bury St Edmunds

CONTENTS

Acknowledgements vi

Introduction 1

1 The political and legislative context 7

2 Collaboration for special educational needs: a national survey 24

3 Collaboration in action 45

4 The organization and management of collaboration 65

5 Resourcing additional needs 76

6 Effective teaching and learning 88

7 Sharing expertise 105

8 The way forward 119

References 133
Index 140

ACKNOWLEDGEMENTS

We wish to express our gratitude to those working in schools and LEAs – headteachers, teachers, SENCOs, governors, advisers and specialist teachers – who gave time to talk to us about their experiences of collaboration.

We would also like to acknowledge the help of Deanne Crowther and Mei Lin at the Special Needs Research Centre, University of Newcastle upon Tyne, who assisted Alan Dyson in carrying out and analysing the national survey, and who contributed to the report which forms Chapter 2.

In addition, we want to thank Gaynor Wingham, who assisted us with interviewing in our five case-study cluster groups.

Thanks also to Alex Crawford, who assisted with proof-reading.

INTRODUCTION

In recent years, there has been increasing concern in many countries that their schools are not enabling pupils to achieve high enough standards. The concern arises not only from the threat to pupils' rights to be educated to take their place in society, but perhaps even more directly, because countries need an effectively educated population to support productivity levels and to achieve economic prosperity (OECD 1995).

It has long been known, for example, that social deprivation has influenced school achievement. Some pupils have appeared – to varying degrees – to be resilient to the deprivational effects of their circumstances, and consequently to have achieved adequate or better attainments in school. However, those made vulnerable by their circumstances have depended on their schools' capacity, and, more importantly, on their schools' concern and willingness to respond to their needs. Modern technology has reduced the employment opportunities for those with low educational levels. As a result, pressure has been put on schools to improve their teaching of these vulnerable pupils. Thus, the problem of lack of employment is conceived of as a problem of the education system, and countries have often shown more concern in trying to make schools more 'effective' in raising standards, than in attempting to reduce social deprivation and its effect on children's vulnerability in more direct ways (Dyson 1997).

The diversity of individual pupils' learning needs also includes those whose vulnerability arises from special educational needs. This term has come increasingly to be used in different countries to refer to children's and young people's disabilities or significant difficulties. The term came into use because of the growing understanding that special educational needs are not just the result of causes within the child or young person. Individuals may be more or less vulnerable or resilient, depending on the interaction between the resources and needs of the individual, and the resources and deficiencies of the environment. There has also been increasing awareness in countries that special educational needs should not debar individuals from the right to take their place in society. This awareness has led to demands that they have a right to be educated in the 'least restrictive environment', in the words of the formulation used in the USA.

The scope for individual schools, and the teachers within them, to meet the diversity of their pupils' needs broadly depends on three main factors. The first is the flexibility of response allowed by the organizational and curricular structures of the education system in which the schools operate. The second is the level of knowledge, skills and understanding to which teachers are trained, and the scope given to teachers to use their abilities to meet the individual pupil's learning and personal needs. The third factor is the level of resources the society in a particular country is willing to allocate to the education of its children and young people. This is mentioned last, since the first two factors largely determine how well any given level of resource can be put to use in meeting the diversity of pupils' needs.

In most countries, education is provided by individual schools, working under the direction of some level of local or regional administration. Any flexibility in responsiveness to pupil need is then dependent on how individual schools and the administrative agencies above them operate. Within most education systems, this arrangement causes a degree of rigidity resulting from the limited scope available to individual schools, and also from the procedural and administrative restrictions which legislation and other constraints impose on the agencies.

Our studies have shown that, in some countries, groups of schools have sought to break through this rigidity, and to increase their scope for responding to their pupils' needs, by collaborating to pool their resources and generally by supporting each other. Some administrative agencies have also recognized the potential advantages of this kind of collaboration between schools, and have put in place measures to encourage it. For example, Meijer (OECD 1997) describes how the Netherlands has set up regional networks of clusters of schools, as a means of encouraging the inclusion of pupils with special educational needs into ordinary schools. Each cluster consists of between 20 and 40 mainstream schools, and about two special schools. A large proportion of funding for special education is allocated to the clusters, and it is then left to the schools as a group to decide how far the mainstream schools will make provision for pupils with learning difficulties, and how far provision will be made in the special schools.

In this book, we consider how collaboration can improve schools' effectiveness in responding to the diversity of their pupils' requirements, focusing on pupils' special educational needs. We deal mainly with practice in the United Kingdom, but we have already mentioned that moves towards collaboration are not confined to this country. The concern to increase schools' responsiveness through collaboration extends the prevailing way of looking at school effectiveness by going beyond the scope available to individual schools. The study of school effectiveness has made a contribution to improving the way that individual schools can operate. However, by taking a broader view of the options available to schools, opportunities open up to permit greater flexibility of response to the diversity of pupils' needs. The previous UK Government's attempts to push up standards of achievement by forcing schools to compete for pupils has in fact not suppressed a willingness to collaborate to varying degrees among a significant number of schools.

Concern for the rights of children and young people has, as we mention above, been one of the main spurs to increase schools' capacity to respond to their pupils' special educational needs. Initially, this concern led to an approach which emphasized the integration of pupils with special educational needs into mainstream schools. The aim was that pupils should accommodate themselves to the way that schools offered education, and that schools should make what efforts they could to 'differentiate the curriculum' to allow for pupils' disabilities and significant difficulties (National Curriculum Council 1989). This conception derived partly from the way that the National Curriculum was presented in terms of a hypothetical sequence of age-based norms within the relevant subjects to be taught. Differentiation was thus regarded as an attempt by teachers to make modifications of their approaches to allow for pupil diversity (Norwich 1996; Lindsay and Thompson 1997).

Thinking in many countries has moved beyond this, based on an awareness that such an approach does not fully meet the concept of children's and young people's rights. UNESCO and the Spanish Government organized a world conference in Salamanca on special needs education in 1994 (UNESCO 1994), at the end of which a statement containing the following was issued:

> We ... reaffirm ... the necessity and urgency of providing education for children, youth and adults with special educational needs within the regular education system ...
> (para. 1)
>
> regular schools with this inclusive orientation ... provide an effective education to the majority of children and improve the efficiency and ultimately cost-effectiveness of the entire education system.
> (para. 2)

As Ainscow (1997) and Wedell (1995) have pointed out, the implications of inclusive education go far beyond the concept of integration. If schools offer inclusive education, they are starting from a different point of departure – for example, recognizing that pupils do not conform to the notional age-based norms of a curriculum. Such schools take as their starting point in planning education, pupils as they are in their locality. They take 'ownership' not only of those pupils who are resilient and can accommodate standard teaching approaches, but also of those who are vulnerable, and who have to be met more than half way. As the Salamanca Statement asserts, such an approach is more likely to offer effective education, since it accepts the reality of the diversity of the learning and personal needs of all pupils within a school. However, the challenge for schools is correspondingly greater.

This challenge is partly recognized in the Green Paper on the education of children and young people with special educational needs (SEN), which the new Labour Government issued for consultation towards the end of 1997 (DfEE 1997b). In the introduction, the Government asserts that it will 'promote the inclusion of children with special educational needs within mainstream schooling wherever possible'. Clearly, the qualification in the latter part of this sentence is significant. It indicates an awareness that the move towards inclusive education is likely to be gradualistic, and that it will affect children differently according

Introduction

to the nature and degree of their special educational needs. A summary of the points raised about the Green Paper, among those participating in an electronic discussion concerned with special needs education, reflects these concerns:

> it was felt that the GP does not sufficiently acknowledge the different degrees of educational challenge which different forms and degrees of special educational needs pose for mainstream schools – and for the pupils themselves.
>
> Parents' wish for inclusive education for their children is countered by doubts whether their children's needs, particularly those with more severe learning needs, will in fact be met in inclusive settings.
>
> (SENCO-forum, 1998)

The previous UK Government's legislative proposals to increase the competitive pressure on schools and to reduce LEAs' funding to support pupils' SENs, resulted in pressure from special needs lobby groups aimed at ensuring support for mainstream schools' efforts to meet their pupils' SENs (Wedell 1996). This led to an extension of the proposed Code of Practice to meet these aims in the final legislation. However, at a period of financial constraint, the necessary support to schools was seriously reduced (Ofsted 1997). Mainstream schools in the UK have been experiencing difficulty in meeting the needs of many pupils. The sharp rise in the proportion of pupils who have been excluded from school is evidence of this (Ofsted 1996a), and indicates how behaviour problems represent an aspect of pupils' special educational needs which pose a particular challenge to mainstream schools. Even the Code of Practice itself has elements which, by introducing procedural aspects to channel support to pupils, potentially constrains schools' flexibility of response and so runs counter to inclusive intentions.

In the following chapters, we examine how collaboration between groupings of schools can help to extend their flexibility in responding to the diversity of their pupils' needs, particularly those pupils who have special educational requirements. We consider these issues in the context of current moves towards inclusive education in the UK and elsewhere.

In Chapter 1, we look at the political and legislative context within which schools' attempts at collaboration occur. Laws and policies can hinder or facilitate collaboration – and can render schools themselves more or less resilient or vulnerable in their attempts to achieve inclusion. The survey of collaborative practice to meet pupils' special educational needs reported in Chapter 2 shows that collaboration in the UK is relatively widespread, but that collaboration occurs in different forms and to different degrees. We describe a few examples of more developed levels of collaboration in Chapter 3, and in Chapter 4 examine the processes which are involved when schools attempt to collaborate more closely.

One of the main influences on collaboration, as we have already mentioned, is the way that schools are able to obtain resources, and to make decisions about their use. This topic is considered separately in Chapter 5. In Chapters 6 and 7, we look at how collaboration has been found to enable schools to become more flexible and effective in meeting their pupils' special educational needs. In Chapter 6, we consider how this is achieved within the schools themselves, and, in Chapter 7, how schools can make better use of specialist support.

Our book is written at a time of new resolve to achieve greater effectiveness in meeting pupils' special educational needs within a policy to promote inclusive education. In Chapter 8, we evaluate the scope that collaboration can offer schools in this developing context.

1
THE POLITICAL AND LEGISLATIVE CONTEXT

INTRODUCTION

In common with many advanced Western economies in the 1980s and 1990s, the education system in the UK was subject to a restructuring which emphasized individuality, parental choice and direct accountability of schools for the use of resources and the standards of education they offer. Ranson (1992) has suggested that, in the UK, a system based on social democratic principles of equity, social responsibility and consensus values within a framework of local political control was replaced with one based on national control of the curriculum, school-based control over finance and management and the introduction of a quasi-market via parental choice of schools. This radical reorganization, which was introduced in order to make the system more 'efficient' and 'effective' and to 'raise standards' has been brought about by a series of legislative changes which have emphasized individual choice, diversity of provision, excellence of outcomes and value for money. Individual schools have been encouraged (some might say 'compelled') to compete for pupils and for resources, so that their energies are focused on the survival of their own institution, and local education authorities' powers are so diminished that some commentators have claimed that they have become 'the authority of last resort. They will have to provide where the market has failed' (Tomlinson 1994).

One group for whom there has been particular concern throughout this transformation has been pupils with special educational needs (SEN), since it has been suggested by a number of commentators that this group will be disadvantaged in a number of ways by the emphasis on high achievement and competition between schools (Wedell 1990; Housden 1993; Evans and Lunt 1994). As Simkins (1994) has pointed out, the (then Conservative) Government was concerned with what they termed 'the three Es: Efficiency, Economy and Effectiveness', but did not address a fourth E – that is, Equity.

This chapter will discuss the changes in the system over the past ten years, current policy initiatives and the impact these are having on the education of pupils with special educational needs.

DEFINING SPECIAL EDUCATIONAL NEEDS

The current definition of special educational needs which operates within the legislation is that originally set out in the 1981 Education Act and reaffirmed in the Code of Practice (DfE 1994a):

> A child has special educational needs if he has a learning difficulty which calls for special educational provision to be made for him.
> (DfE 1993, Section 156)

This definition then hinges on the definition of 'learning difficulty':

> significantly greater difficulty in learning than the majority of children of his age
>
> having a disability which prevents or hinders him from making use of facilities of a kind generally provided in schools within the area
>
> if under five, likely to fall into one of these categories when over that age
> (DfE 1993, Section 156)

and 'special educational provision':

> provision which is additional to or otherwise different from the educational provision made generally for children of the child's age in maintained schools, other than special schools, in the area
> (DfE 1993)

for children under two 'special educational provision' is:

> educational provision of any kind
> (DfE 1993, Section 156)

This definition was replicated and persists in the 1993 and 1996 Acts and in the recent Green Paper on special education (DfEE 1997b).

The vagueness of the definition and its relativity in relation to local standards of achievement and provision made it impossible to operationalize in any coherent fashion across the country (Audit Commission 1992a). Even within LEAs, there was, and continues to be, a wide variety of policy and practice. The fragmentation of LEAs through the introduction of LMS and GM status has exacerbated this variation (Fish and Evans 1995).

In practice, there are as many definitions of special educational needs as there are schools and LEAs. One of the major problems confronting those who wish to make policy and to plan provision is the lack of consensus among professionals, parents and policy makers about what constitutes a special educational need and what level of provision any particular need requires. At the risk of adding to the confusion, we are using the term in this book to describe levels and types of need which lead schools to make special provision for a child or to allocate extra resources to that child, or to call for extra resources from the LEA. These levels and types might correspond to the stages described in the Code of Practice for identifying pupils with SEN (DfE 1994a). It is important to emphasize that the majority of children with special educational needs (as defined by above) are educated in mainstream schools. The proportion of children with special educational needs in mainstream schools varies, but can be between 10 and 40 per cent, depending on the socio-economic make-up of the school population. The more socially disadvantaged the school community is, the more likely it is to have a relatively high proportion of pupils with special educational needs (Mortimore and Whitty 1997).

The current proportion of children with more severe needs who are being educated in special schools is around 1.3 per cent of the total school population (Norwich 1997). There is also a growing number of children who have difficulties with schooling, who are being excluded from schools and receiving some kind of part-time provision (DfEE 1997b). Technically (according to the definition in the legislation) these children do not *necessarily* have special educational needs (although many have statements of needs (Ofsted 1996a)). However, it could be argued that children, whose behaviour is such that schools cannot cope with them, have learning difficulties which arise from social and emotional problems and that they are casualties of a more market-driven approach to education which is stressing high standards of achievement and conformity to a narrower range of standards of behaviour (Skrtic 1991). The Green Paper on special education (DfEE 1997b) acknowledges the scale of the problem by devoting a complete chapter to the problems of children with emotional and behavioural difficulties.

THE 'MARKET' APPROACH TO EDUCATION

The White Paper which preceded the 1993 Education Act (DfE 1992) clearly articulated the principles upon which it was founded: quality; diversity; increased parental choice; greater autonomy for schools; and, greater accountability. Thus, the legislation which followed continued the trend which had been set by the 1988 and 1992 Acts: decentralization of responsibility for the management and delivery of education to schools accompanied by centralization of decision-making about the curriculum and monitoring of standards to the national level.

A key feature of the earlier legislation (the 1988 Act) was the introduction of formula-funding of schools along with more open enrolment, which, in effect, set up a quasi-market by tying the funding of schools to the number of pupils they could attract (Gewirtz *et al.* 1995; Levačić 1995; Whitty *et al.* 1998). The formulae which LEAs had to construct to fund schools were to be based predominantly on 'pupils numbers weighted for age' (AWPUs – age-weighted pupil units), according to Circular 7/88 (DES 1988) which laid out the principles of formula funding. Later, this was modified to encompass 'pupil-related factors' which included some weighting for special educational needs (up to 5 per cent). But, however it was calculated, the principle was that schools would rely for at least 75 per cent of their funding on the numbers of pupils they could attract. Thus schools had an incentive to enrol the maximum number of pupils in order to maximize their income.

However, in order for the market to operate effectively, the 'consumers' or 'choosers' of schools would need information on which to base their choices. So, the Government set up structures to give parents information. These included the establishment of a system of testing pupils at the ages of 7, 11, 14 and 16 and publishing league tables of the results of these tests. Thus, it was assumed that parents would choose the most successful schools, and less successful schools would be forced to raise their standards in order to compete. Many commentators have argued that raw test scores are not a good indicator of the effectiveness of schools (Goldstein *et al.* 1996; *Observer* 1997), and that 'value-added' scores would be a fairer way of presenting the results. The present Labour Government is sympathetic to this argument and is committed to introduce 'value-added' scores alongside the raw data to be published. However, much research on parental choice of schools indicates that choosing a school is not the unidimensional super-rational phenomenon that policy-makers have tended to assume (Gewirtz *et al.* 1995; West *et al.* 1995; Adler 1997). Different groups of parents make choices based on different criteria. The aptly titled '"Happiness" as a criterion of parental choice of school' (Coldron and Boulton 1991) sums up this complexity. Gewirtz *et al.* (1995) argue that middle-class 'cosmopolitan' parents tend to choose within a wider circuit of schools than working-class 'local' choosers. The key criteria for 'local' choosers are concerned with safety, distance and convenience. The cosmopolitan choosers are more concerned with exam results and discipline, and are more willing to let their children travel further to school. Both groups of parents are concerned about those with whom their children will mix at school. Thus, for some parents, 'value-added' test results may be of less importance than raw scores, because the raw scores are an indicator of the social mix of the school since, to some extent, they reflect the social composition of the school population.

Evans and Vincent (1997) have argued that parents of children with special needs are also differentially active within the quasi-market. Some are more competent choosers than others, and the social class of parents can be an empowering or a disempowering factor for these parents also. This argument will be developed further in a later section of this chapter.

Another example of the increased amount of information parents will have when choosing schools is the inspection report prepared by Ofsted inspectors. This is available to any parent who wishes to see it, and its findings are often publicized in the local newpaper. Again, these may be differentially used by parents in different social groups. It is likely that only the most literate parents will obtain and read the reports of all the schools in which they are interested. However, it is likely that schools with good Ofsted reports will publicize these through the local press and will mention them in their school prospectuses and that schools with bad reports may find that these generate bad publicity, so that, even if the precise content of the reports is not known by parents when they are making choices, an overall impression (either favourable or unfavourable) can be created.

Although the 1988 Act gave the majority of parents the right to 'express a preference' for the school of their choice, such rights for parents of children with statements of special educational needs were not given until the enactment of the 1993 legislation. Prior to this, parents of children with statements had the right to be consulted, and the placement of a child with a statement in a mainstream school was to be 'subject to the wishes of his parents', but the rights of parents of children with statements to choose a school for their child have always been somewhat circumscribed. Even under current legislation, mainstream placement of a child with a statement is subject to the provisos of 'efficient use of resources', 'the needs of the child being met' and 'the education of other children in the school not being compromised'. Thus parents with children who have special educational needs are disadvantaged within the educational marketplace for a number of reasons which will be discussed in more detail below.

One of the key principles of the 1993 Act was to encourage 'diversity' in schools. By this, the Government meant that schools should be encouraged to become grant-maintained (GM) – to leave the overall policy and resourcing framework of their local authority and be managed entirely by locally elected and appointed governors – and that GM schools should further diversify by focusing on a particular curricular area (for example, IT or languages) and by selecting a proportion of their pupils on the basis of ability. Research by Halpin *et al.* (1997) casts doubt on the diversification thesis. They found that GM schools tended to become more conservative and narrower in their conceptualization of what an effective school should be. They had introduced a more traditional uniform code (i.e. ties and blazers for boys and girls) and a more traditional curriculum, stressing academic excellence as a primary goal. There are no examples in their research of GM schools which have pioneered innovative curricula or teaching methods. One result of this new traditionalism appears to have been that GM schools are less tolerant of special educational needs and emotional and behavioural problems. A knock-on effect of this is that remaining LEA schools, in competition with GM schools, have felt obliged to follow their lead and to adopt stricter uniform codes and to underplay their efforts on behalf of children with special educational needs (see Evans and Vincent 1997).

A key factor in these changes has been the role of governors. In GM schools, foundation and parent governors are in a majority. In LEA-maintained schools, there are still governors appointed by the local authority. Nevertheless, in both types of school, the remit and responsibility of governors is to maintain the viability of their school. They are not obliged to be interested in the impact of the market in schooling on other schools in the local area, or on the education of children other than those in their school. Thus, the role of the LEA in trying to ensure an overall level of quality of education for the whole community has been undermined by local management of schools and the setting up of GM schools.

THE IMPACT OF THE REFORMS ON CHILDREN WITH SPECIAL EDUCATIONAL NEEDS

When the market reforms of education and the National Curriculum were first introduced, many commentators warned that they would have an adverse effect on the education of children with SEN. The arguments centred around the contention that the market would favour those who had the most social advantages – middle-class and well-educated parents whose children appeared well-motivated and able – and that schools, if they were in the fortunate position of being over-subscribed, would choose those pupils who would be least problematic and least resource-intensive to educate (Bowe *et al.* 1992; Evans and Lunt 1994; Fish and Evans 1995). That is, they would be less inclined to choose pupils with special educational needs and socially disadvantaged pupils. Ranson sums up this aspect of the marketization of schooling:

> The market is formally neutral, yet substantively interested ... Yet, of course, the market masks its social bias. It elides, but reproduces the inequalities which consumers bring to the market place. Under the guise of neutrality, the institution of the market actively confirms and reinforces the pre-existing social order of wealth, privilege and prejudice. The market, let it be clear, is a crude mechanism of social selection and is intended as such.
>
> (Ranson 1992, p. 72)

There has always been a market in education. The more privileged and more socially-skilled parents have always been able to obtain a more favourable education for their children, by paying for it, by taking advantage of scholarships and assisted places or by moving into the catchment area of their desired school (Evans and Vincent 1997). Some parents of children with special educational needs have also been able to 'play the market' successfully and been able to obtain extra resources or placement in expensive special educational establishments by using their cultural capital for the benefit of their children (Riddell and Brown 1994; Gross 1996). Some parents have successfully challenged the decisions made by the LEAs about the level or type of resources allocated to their children with SEN, either through the courts, or by appealing to the Tribunal set up to hear such cases in 1994. The majority of appeals have come from parents whose children have specific learning difficulties, and who, it is assumed, are articulate and well-educated and able to use the system in this way. Thus, the less favoured parents, in this respect, are less able to obtain extra resources for their children.

As Ranson argues, the current system exacerbates this tendency. Recent research, both in the UK and the USA has indicated that, when parental choice is unfettered, schools become more socially stratified (Glatter *et al.* 1997). The result of this is increased exclusion of troublesome pupils, and the creation of 'sink' schools, where the majority of pupils are socially disadvantaged or have special educational needs (for example, the Ridings School in Halifax, which became notorious in 1996 after it was named the 'worst school in England'). It was clear that, in this locality, the market had produced a distinct hierarchy of schools, with GM and independent schools attracting a higher achieving group of children, and with one or two less favoured schools experiencing falling rolls and low exam results (*Guardian* 1996).

In a less dramatic fashion, this pattern is being repeated in many areas, particularly in urban areas, where there are a number of competing schools within travelling distance for most children and where there are wide variations in socio-economic circumstances in populations living in close proximity to each other. League tables for London Boroughs, for example, show schools with widely differing GCSE results within LEAs covering a relatively small geographical area. In shire counties, such extreme variations are less common, so, for example, the range of results in North-east Hampshire schools is 27–68 per cent A* to C (ten LEA comprehensive schools). In Camden, the range is 12–71 per cent (11 LEA and GM comprehensive schools). The average scores for the two LEAs were 48 per cent A* to C in Camden and 49 per cent in Hampshire (*Guardian* 18 November 1997). In addition, the cross-over between LEAs is more marked in Metropolitan Boroughs, so that some LEAs import large numbers of children across their boundaries and schools no longer relate in any meaningful way to their neighbourhood communities, whereas in rural and semi-rural areas, lack of transport means that such movement across areas is less likely.

Thus, Ranson argues:

> The Conservatives' education reforms have sought to replace the post-war 'social democratic' tradition with the principle of the market place supported by power concentrated in Whitehall. Markets, however, will only fragment local communities, while centralised power engenders inertia.
>
> (Ranson 1994: ix)

He goes on to develop his vision for 'a learning society', which:

> should enable parents to become as committed to their own continuing development as they are to that of their children; men and women should be able to assert their right to learn as well as to support the family; learning co-operatives should be formed at work and in community centres.
>
> (Ranson 1994: ix)

This is a vision of an inclusive education system which:

> has, as its foundation, a strong system of local democracy that allows citizens from many backgrounds to play an active part in developing their communities, including the educational institutions which meet their needs. Only such a new moral and political order can provide the foundation for sustaining the personal development of all.
>
> (Ranson 1994: ix)

THE EDUCATIONAL FRAMEWORK

Currently, as Ranson has described, the educational system of England and Wales is a combination of extreme decentralization (local management of schools (LMS) and local management of special schools (LMSS)) and extreme centralization (National Curriculum, National Testing arrangements and Ofsted Inspections). The role of the 'intermediate tier' (Tomlinson 1994) (i.e. the local authority) has been greatly reduced. In addition, a number of Quangos (quasi-autonomous non-governmental organizations), often called 'agencies', have taken over some of the functions which used to be performed by locally elected democratic bodies at local or regional level. These include: the Funding Agency for Schools (FAS), which has taken over some of the LEAs' planning and funding responsibilities (the FAS is to be wound up under the 1998 Education Act); Ofsted, which has taken over some of the LEAs' inspection and monitoring roles (although proposals in the White Paper, *Excellence in Schools* (DfEE 1997a) will give the LEAs a role in target setting for individual schools); the SEN Tribunals, which deal with appeals against LEA decisions in the statutory assessment process for SEN; and, governing bodies, which include some members elected by teachers in the school and by parents, but others who are appointed by local and diocesan authorities and others who are co-opted. Tomlinson (1994) has called this proliferation of agencies and boards 'the new magistracy'.

The Labour Government has said that it will continue with this framework. It stated in a White Paper published soon after taking office that its interest was in 'standards not structures' (DfEE 1997a). Thus local management of schools (including special schools) would continue relatively unchanged, although GM schools would be brought back under LEA control in the guise of 'foundation' schools. Admissions arrangements are to be set up according to a Code of Practice which would be published by the Secretary of State. There is to be a 'local forum' consisting of headteacher or governor, representatives from the various schools in the LEA and representatives from the LEA itself. The local forum would be 'the main representative vehicle for discussion and communication between different admissions authorities and schools', but it 'would not take binding decisions' (DfEE 1997a). Thus, the governing bodies of the former GM schools (foundation schools) and aided schools would be responsible for admissions to those schools, the LEA would be responsible for admissions to 'community' schools. The 'Greenwich judgement', which confirmed that LEAs and schools were not permitted to give preference to children living within the LEA boundary, was not to be reversed. Thus, the key building blocks of the quasi-market in education – open enrolment and per capita funding of schools – will continue unchanged. The only restriction to be placed on schools was that they were not to be allowed to operate partial selection by ability. It would seem that, under 'New Labour', the inequalities built into the school system would remain.

The role of LEAs is to be enhanced, but it is as a monitor, rather than a provider, that LEAs would operate. Since local government reorganization, there are now 150 local authorities, many of them new creations, which will be setting up their own policies and structures for the administration of education. Many of the new unitary authorities are relatively small (for example, Berkshire has been split into six separate authorities), and the tendency has been to try to relate local authorities more closely to the communities they serve. It is yet to be seen how this will affect the responsiveness of LEAs to the educational aspirations of their local populations.

THE CURRENT SITUATION FOR SEN PROVISION

The current framework of SEN provision is widely divergent across the country. There are wide variations in the proportion of children given statements from less than 2 per cent in some LEAs to over 4 per cent in others (DfEE 1997b). There are also variations in the proportions educated in special as opposed to mainstream schools. In some LEAs, under 0.5 per cent of children are in special schools. In others the proportion is over 2 per cent (DfEE 1997b). The Green Paper, *Excellence for All Children* (DfEE 1997b), calls for suggestions to try to reduce the proportion of children with statements and to increase the numbers of children with SEN being educated in inclusive settings. However, there are powerful countervailing forces against realizing these aspirations.

The focus on 'standards' being promoted by the Labour Government has led to the 'naming and shaming' of schools which the Ofsted inspectors have deemed to be failing. Some of these have been special schools, and others, schools in areas of extreme social deprivation. There is increasing evidence that, to avoid such public humiliation, many secondary schools are concentrating on improving levels of attainment on the C/D boundary, and putting fewer resources into supporting pupils with lower levels of attainment (Gewirtz *et al*. 1995). Their research gave several examples of schools which had cut the numbers of SEN teachers in order to focus resources elsewhere. At the same time, the full implementation of the Code of Practice (DfE 1994a) is an added pressure on schools and has led to an increase in the numbers of pupils identified as having SEN and the requirement to make proper provision for them. One of the outcomes of these increased pressures is that the numbers of pupils with statements is rising at an increasing rate. The numbers of pupils with statements in mainstream schools has almost doubled since 1991 (*TES* 24 October 1997). This is not due to a large rise in the inclusion of pupils who would formerly have been in special schools, but to the pressure which parents and schools are exerting on LEAs to obtain extra resources for children with learning difficulties in mainstream. The operation of the Code of Practice (DfE 1994a) has ensured that pupils with SEN are identified and registered. Some LEAs are channelling extra funding for SEN to mainstream schools through an 'audit' system which also enhances schools' motivation to identify and seek resources to support children with SEN. However, the Government is concerned about the amount of resources tied up in producing and maintaining statements and has stated in the Green Paper, *Excellence for All Children* (DfEE 1997b), that it is looking for strategies to reduce the statement rate.

Another apparent consequence of the more rigorous attainment targets and public accountability through league tables and Ofsted inspections is a large increase in the numbers of children permanently excluded from schools. The increase is particularly marked in the primary sector (Parsons 1996). The total number of children permanently excluded rose by 13 per cent in 1995/6 to a figure of 12,500. The rise in primary-aged pupils excluded was 18 per cent (1400). A range of explanations has been offered for this, but, whatever the causes, it is clear that strategies need to be found to enable schools to cope with the increased challenges posed by some pupils. The White Paper, *Excellence in Schools* (DfEE 1997a), suggests that the 'behaviour support plans' required to be formulated by LEAs under the 1997 Act will lead to a more effective multi-agency approach to support good discipline and behaviour at the local level. This appears to be a recognition of the fact that school exclusions are a community problem and not one which can be tackled by schools on their own, without effective support from other local agencies, including other schools.

THE ROLE OF COLLABORATION IN INCREASING THE EFFECTIVENESS OF SCHOOLS

We have argued that the increased competitiveness between schools engendered by the framework of LMS and open enrolment, which has made schools more sensitive about their reputation and status within their local communities (and beyond), has led to less tolerance by some schools of children with learning and behaviour difficulties. It has also led to a scarcity of resources and expertise, since LEA support teams have been wound down, as delegation of resources to schools has increased. The funding of individual pupils, through statements and through 'audits' linked to the Code of Practice, has led to an ethos in which learning and behaviour difficulties are seen as problems to be tackled by schools in isolation and not a community or LEA responsibility. This is part of a wider ethos in which 'school effectiveness' is seen as a matter for individual schools to promote by training and enhancing the capabilities of their staff. Such strategies do not usually include collaboration with other schools, although there are exceptions to this (Weston *et al.* 1992).

The White Paper, *Excellence in Schools* (DfEE 1997a), and the Green Paper, *Excellence for All Children* (DfEE 1997b), give a more positive message about the role of LEAs and local communities in promoting collaboration, rather than competition, between schools. For example, the White Paper calls for the setting up of an 'Early Years Forum' in each locality to plan the provision of education for pre-school children. This is a positive move away from a market-driven system, funded by vouchers, to a collaborative system involving private and public providers, coordinated by the LEA. Another initiative is 'Education Action Zones' which will be set up in areas with a mix of under-performing schools in areas of high social disadvantage. These Zones would consist of '2 or 3 secondary schools, with supporting primaries and associated SEN provision' (DfEE 1997a). The Government expects the Action Zones:

> to operate on the basis of an action forum which will include parents and other representatives from the local business and social community, as well as representatives from the constituent schools and the LEA. The Forum would draw up an action programme, including targets for each participating school and the Zone as a whole.
> (DfEE 1997a, para. 8: 39)

Again, this marks a move away from the market as a means of coordination and action, to a more comprehensive and considered method of decision-making about provision. Local schools and local people are expected, in this vision, to act together to improve the quality of education in their area.

The White Paper also talks about 'families of schools', which will be supported by specialist schools within their family. Thus 'a key to the Department's selection of schools for support as specialist schools will be commitment to the wider community'. It suggests that 'families of schools will want to consider what type of sharing between themselves and with the community suits their needs best'. This concept of 'families' of schools is similar to that of the 'cluster', first suggested in the ILEA report on special education (ILEA 1985), in that it proposes groupings of schools which will share expertise and resources to enable them to meet the needs of their local population.

The Green Paper, *Excellence for All Children* (DfEE 1997b), is also concerned about structures to facilitate cooperation between groups of schools. It acknowledges that competition between schools and worries about a school's standing in the league tables has been detrimental to the inclusion of pupils with special educational needs. It suggests, in the section on 'increasing inclusion', that special school staff could be enabled to work more closely with mainstream schools and support services to meet the needs of all pupils with SEN. It continues:

> We want to build on existing good practice. Possible ways forward are:
>
> Guidance to LEAs and schools on co-operative working. This might cover:
> - shared facilities;
> - shared teaching and non-teaching expertise;
> - support for pupils who move between special and mainstream schools;
> - special schools becoming part of cluster arrangements with primary and secondary schools;
> - suggesting that LEAs include in their Education Development Plans (EDPs) arrangements for collaboration within the framework of generally inclusive provision, including targets for improvement. LEA plans should reflect any arrangements agreed at regional level and would be subject to inspection by Ofsted;
> - extending LEAs' duty to review the provision they make for pupils with SEN to include a requirement to review collaborative arrangements between schools;
> - placing a requirement on special and mainstream schools to provide details of their collaborative arrangements in their annual reports. For special schools, this could include setting targets for the amount of time pupils should participate in mainstream education.
>
> (DfEE 1997b, pp. 50–1)

The White and Green Papers have acknowledged that the 'market' is not the ideal way to coordinate an education system, although, as discussed above, many of the market mechanisms established by the 1988, 1992 and 1993 Acts remain in place. However, the current Labour Government proposes to attempt to mitigate some of the negative consequences of the current system by introducing 'an intermediate tier' of discussion and decision making between the school and the national level. This will include, not only the LEA, but also a number of other key institutions in the local area. Thus, the concept of local democracy is extended, in order to provide representation of a wider group of local interests and views in local forums.

It has been demonstrated, by argument and by research, that an unfettered market in education produces outcomes which are inequitable. Children who are likely to require extra resources, or who may not perform well in school, or whose parents are less effective choosers may not always obtain the education they require. Resources may be diverted from the most needy children to those whose parents are most able to influence the school or local authority to provide them (as Riddell and Brown 1994 and Gross 1996 have shown). Lee (1996) in his book *The Search for Equity* has argued that 'equity' is very difficult to achieve, but that the current system of resourcing schools through formula-funding produces highly inequitable results. The sharing of resources and expertise across schools would be one way of reducing some of these inequities. It would also provide a way in which communities could ensure that all the children in the community could be adequately educated within their local schools, and would give community members the responsibility for ensuring that all local schools were performing well. The present Government's proposals to include independent schools in local networks would add an extra dimension to this.

Apart from considerations of equity and community responsibility, the sharing of resources across schools also answers another of the Government's imperatives – the efficient and effective use of scarce resources. Small schools, in partnerships, are able to access resources which would otherwise be beyond their means. For example, small primary schools can make use of the facilities and expertise available in larger primaries or secondary schools. There are numerous examples of this in the area of curriculum development. Sharing resources leads to economies of scale, so that small schools acting jointly could, for example, employ a Special Educational Needs Coordinator (SENCO) who would work across a number of schools. Many GM schools have received significant extra resources, which have been diverted from LEA funds, which have diminished the pool of funds left for LEA schools. If these resources could be shared across a locality it would enhance the efficiency of the use of funds in the local area.

Recently published league tables (*Observer*, 23 November 1997) have used 'value-added' measures to indicate which secondary schools are most effective as educational institutions. There are still many arguments about the best way of calculating 'added value'; nevertheless, the tables give some indication that some schools in disadvantaged areas are very effective and that schools in more affluent areas, although they may produce very good GCSE results, are not necessarily the most effective schools. Of course, there are some schools, both in advantaged and disadvantaged areas which are not effective, and the isolation of schools in competition with each other will not enhance the overall effectiveness of the education system. If those schools which are effective are encouraged to support the less effective schools, and if parents can see that all schools in a locality are operating effectively and 'adding value', despite differences in their overall GCSE or other results, then the most negative aspects of competition between schools could be mitigated.

CONCLUSION

This book will attempt to demonstrate the educational and social advantages of close collaboration between schools for all pupils, but more especially for those with special educational needs. It will give examples and case studies of effective collaboration and its positive effects. It will discuss ways in which effective collaboration can be achieved. It will review the role of support services and how these can be linked into groups of schools. It will discuss ways of funding special educational needs which will provide a framework for the effective and efficient use of resources by groups of schools, who will make collaborative decisions about which children need support and how this should be organized.

The book ends with a look into the future and discusses the issues which policy makers and practitioners will be grappling with in their attempts to provide the best possible education for all our children in the new millennium.

2

COLLABORATION FOR SPECIAL EDUCATIONAL NEEDS: A NATIONAL SURVEY

Over the last few years, we have begun to learn a great deal about how collaborating groups of schools work, what problems they encounter and what possibilities they open up for the organization of special educational needs provision. The research reported elsewhere in this book and in previous work by the same team (Lunt *et al.* 1994), together with accounts written by teachers and LEA officers (in, for instance, Gains 1994; Ranson and Tomlinson 1994; Macbeth *et al.* 1995; Bridges and Husbands 1996) has begun to create an extensive knowledge base on which future developments can be built. However, almost all of what we know comes from studies of particular cases of collaboration that have in some way come to the notice of researchers or have promoted themselves as being worthy of attention. Not surprisingly, such cases tend to be formally organized, highly active and, in many instances, supported by LEA policy. But are such cases typical? Do other forms of collaboration exist? If so, are they equally formal and dynamic? Is there a range of collaborative practices – and if so, where do the groupings we already know about fit into that range?

The obvious way to answer these questions is to carry out a national survey of collaborative groups, and it is such a survey which is reported in the remainder of this chapter. However, 'national surveys' are of many kinds, and it is important that the reader is clear as to what was and was not attempted here. A full national survey would involve the identification of every cluster group in the country – or at least of a representative sample of such groups. However, there are real difficulties in this task. It is no longer always possible to find LEA personnel who have an overview of collaborative practices in their area and can direct researchers authoritatively towards representative examples. If, on the other hand, cluster groups are to be asked to nominate themselves, how can they be persuaded to do this, given all the other demands on teachers' time, and how can we be sure that those groups which do nominate themselves are representative of all collaborative arrangements? Moreover, underlying all these difficulties is the problem of definition. In order to identify the full range of cluster groupings, we need to know what that range looks like. But how do we know what that range looks like until we have carried out a survey? Considering the focus on particular types of clusters in previous research, this 'chicken and egg' problem is far from purely academic.

THE SURVEY

Given these difficulties, the strategy we adopted was to attempt to construct a sample of cluster groups that would be sufficiently large and diverse that it would have a good chance of covering most, if not all, of the current range of collaborative practices. In other words, rather than attempting the almost impossible task of identifying every cluster group, or even of ensuring that our sample represented the distribution of cluster groups across LEAs, we concentrated on ensuring that as many different types of cluster as possible would be present in our sample. We did this by using a mixture of third-party and self-nomination. We invited the chief education officer (and, where that failed, the principal educational psychologist) in English and Welsh LEAs to nominate a sample of cluster groups to reflect the range of practice in their areas. (The only exceptions were those LEAs where cluster groups had already been investigated by the London Institute team.) In addition, we invited clusters to nominate themselves directly by placing advertisements in the journals of the principal headteacher unions and the National Association of Special Educational Needs. Every nominated cluster was invited to complete a detailed questionnaire. Drawing on the dimensions for describing inter-school collaboration developed by Lunt *et al.* (1994), the questionnaire asked for information on the cluster's origin, composition, extent of collaboration, focus, funding and resultant form of SEN provision. It also asked for information on the management structures supporting the cluster group. Approximately one quarter of the questionnaire responses were followed up by telephone interview in order to clarify and amplify the information that had been provided.

Throughout, we used a very broad definition of 'clusters' ('groupings of schools which have a commitment to share some aspect of their resourcing or decision-making in respect of special educational needs') and encouraged potential respondents who were nevertheless in doubt as to whether their practice 'qualified' to return our questionnaire. Our reasoning was that we needed to identify the widest possible range of practice before we could determine authoritatively what we should and should not regard as a cluster.

The survey took place during the 1995/6 academic year. In the event, completed questionnaires were received from 93 cluster groups across 45 LEA areas. In the remainder of this chapter, we shall attempt to delineate the characteristics of these groups. From time to time, we shall present quantitative as well as qualitative data where we feel that trends within our sample may reflect a national pattern. However, readers are advised to bear in mind the nature of our sample and to treat such data with the caution they deserve.

THE PREVALENCE OF CLUSTER GROUPS

The LEAs from which clusters responded were of all types – shire counties, metropolitan authorities, former ILEA authorities – and were drawn from all geographical areas. Given the number and diversity of these LEAs, we can say with some confidence that clustering is a widespread phenomenon which is not necessarily dependent on particular features of educational geography (such as the proximity of schools in urban areas or the absence of inter-school competition in rural areas). Indeed, it may be even more widespread than our figures suggest. In at least three cases, cluster groups nominated themselves from LEAs which had definitively informed us that they had no clusters; it is entirely possible, therefore, that similar 'hidden' clusters exist elsewhere. Moreover, some LEAs reported that, although they currently had no clusters, they were actively exploring the possibility of establishing some in the near future while others again only established clusters after the survey was complete. It may well be, therefore, that not only is collaboration in cluster groups widespread, but it is also on the increase.

This hypothesis is supported to some extent by the data which we collected on the longevity of cluster groups. The majority (just under 60 per cent) had been established within the last five years (i.e. from 1990 onwards), and might be seen as a response to the new situation created by the 1988 Education Reform Act. In particular, a number of groups reported that they had been established recently in response to the demands placed on mainstream schools by the Code of Practice (DfE 1994a). There is, therefore, some evidence that recent developments have acted as a catalyst for schools to work together. What we cannot tell from a survey of existing groups, of course, is the rate of attrition which clusters experience. Nevertheless, some 40 per cent of cluster groups in the sample had been in existence for more than five years, and almost 7 per cent for more than ten years. Indeed, two groups reported that they had been in existence for over 20 years and a number claimed to have evolved from previous collaborative arrangements such as TVEI consortia. If nothing else, this indicates that cluster groups are capable of surviving for lengthy periods of time and that those groups which have emerged in response to recent developments will not necessarily disappear in the near future.

Cluster groups were more or less evenly distributed in respect of whether they had originated as a 'top-down' (i.e. LEA-led) initiative, a 'bottom-up' (i.e. school-led) initiative, or as the result of a school-LEA partnership. In some areas, of course, it is LEA policy to organize schools into clusters; however, even where this was not the case, it was not unusual to find that the LEA supported their development by providing pump-priming funds or servicing the cluster through administrative or teaching support. On the other hand, LEA support appears not to be a *sine qua non* of cluster development; we were also able to identify a number of cluster groups which had developed without such support and, which, in some cases, had emerged in the teeth of LEA opposition.

THE SIZE AND COMPOSITION OF CLUSTER GROUPS

Respondents were asked to report the numbers of schools in their cluster groups. Just under three-quarters of clusters comprised ten schools or fewer with a quarter comprising fewer than six schools. Only a few clusters (10 per cent) had more than 15 schools – the largest of these comprising some 61 primary schools in a single LEA. To a certain extent, it is possible to see in this pattern a 'natural' limit to the size of a cluster, though the existence of very large groups indicates that this limit is not absolute. As we shall see, the larger clusters tended to manage issues of size by creating formal management structures and procedures.

Schools do not, of course, select their partners for collaborative activities on a purely arbitrary basis; rather, they tend to have something in common with their partners. As Figure 2.1 indicates, the majority (70 per cent) of clusters in this survey served the same geographical area, while a sizeable minority (over 40 per cent) formed a pyramid of one or more secondary schools and their feeder primaries. It is, however, impossible to say that any one feature is essential for the formation of clusters; many groups did not serve a single area or form a pyramid but had something else in common. They might, for instance, take the form of a consortium of special schools or a group of denominational schools. Similarly, same-phase and cross-phase clusters were about evenly represented. Interestingly, less than 20 per cent of responding clusters were based on special school 'catchment' areas. Given the long-standing advocacy of special schools as centres of excellence and expertise – an advocacy renewed in the recent Green Paper (DfEE 1997b) – this is a somewhat surprising finding which suggests that there is a good deal of work to be done before collaboration between special and mainstream schools becomes a reality.

One issue which emerges from the characteristics of responding clusters is the extent to which we currently have a good definition of what counts as a cluster. One response, for instance, came from a group of Pupil Referral Units and described their relationships with their 'feeder' schools. Another came from an association of home and hospital teaching services. A third came from a school which, paradoxically, claimed not to belong to a cluster but which nevertheless went on to describe a high level of collaboration between all the schools in a small authority in respect of SEN policy. None of these is a cluster in the 'classic' sense of a group of schools (i.e. as opposed to an LEA) sharing resourcing and decision making. On the other hand, they all represent educational organizations working together collaboratively in order to enhance provision for pupils with special educational needs. Pragmatically, we have taken the view that any form of collaboration which could effectively be described through the categories in our questionnaire should be counted as a cluster. Theoretically, we believe that the diversity of responses casts doubt on any hard-and-fast distinction between clusters and other forms of collaboration. This is an issue to which we shall return below.

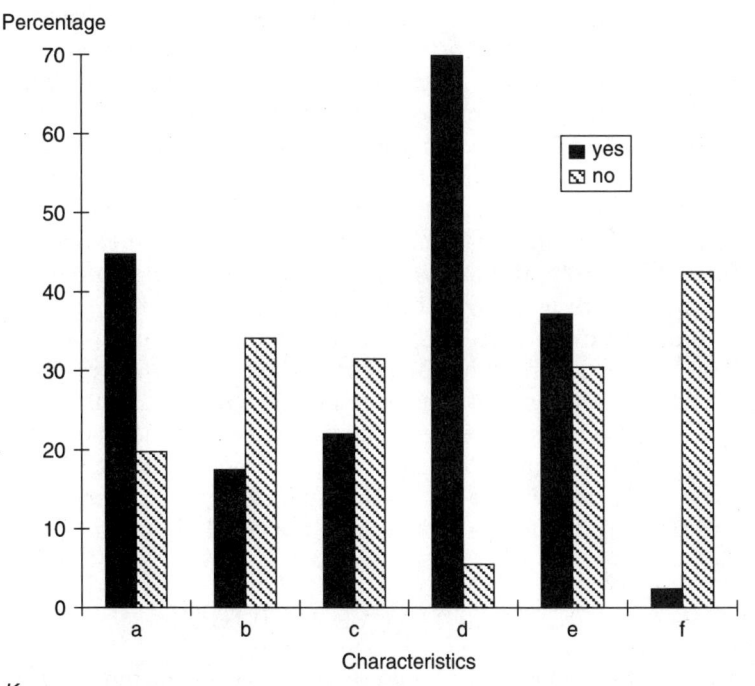

Key:
a = form a pyramid
b = form the catchment area of a participating special school(s)
c = constitute an administrative sub-division of the LEA
d = serve a distinct geographical area
e = belong to the same phase
f = denominational schools

Figure 2.1 Characteristics shared by clustering schools

CLUSTER FOCI

The clusters in our survey had a wide range of concerns. Over half focused exclusively or principally on special needs provision. However, over a third had some other focus and saw special needs simply as one among a range of concerns; many pyramids, for instance, collaborated across a range of issues to do with exchanging information, sharing expertise and developing common policies. Insofar as they were concerned with special needs issues, however, clusters were usually concerned with all pupils with special educational needs in participating schools, rather than with some particular sub-group.

A few clusters, on the other hand, did have a more specific focus. One cluster, for instance, consisted of a group of schools for pupils with severe learning difficulties. Another had been designated by the LEA as a resource for pupils with specific learning difficulties; pupils were referred to the cluster from other primary schools in the LEA and accepted or not according to agreed criteria. The cluster then made available additional teacher support for these pupils funded from their statements. A third cluster comprised a pyramid providing integrated provision for pupils with learning difficulties.

In almost every case, clusters reported that they had played a large part in determining the focus of their own activities. Even where, as above, clusters had been initiated by the LEA as part of its SEN policy, clusters tended to operate with a high level of autonomy. This perhaps reflected a recognition by LEAs that, while they might take the lead in establishing clusters, they could not and should not attempt to determine the detail of their practices.

COLLABORATIVE ACTIVITIES

The questionnaire asked respondents to characterize their clusters' activities in two ways: in terms of the sort and extent of collaboration in which participating schools engaged; and in terms of the sorts of provision which the cluster made for pupils with special educational needs. As Figure 2.2 indicates, schools tended to collaborate in a wide range of ways. The commonest of these involved exchanging information, developing common approaches and participating in joint INSET, though many schools

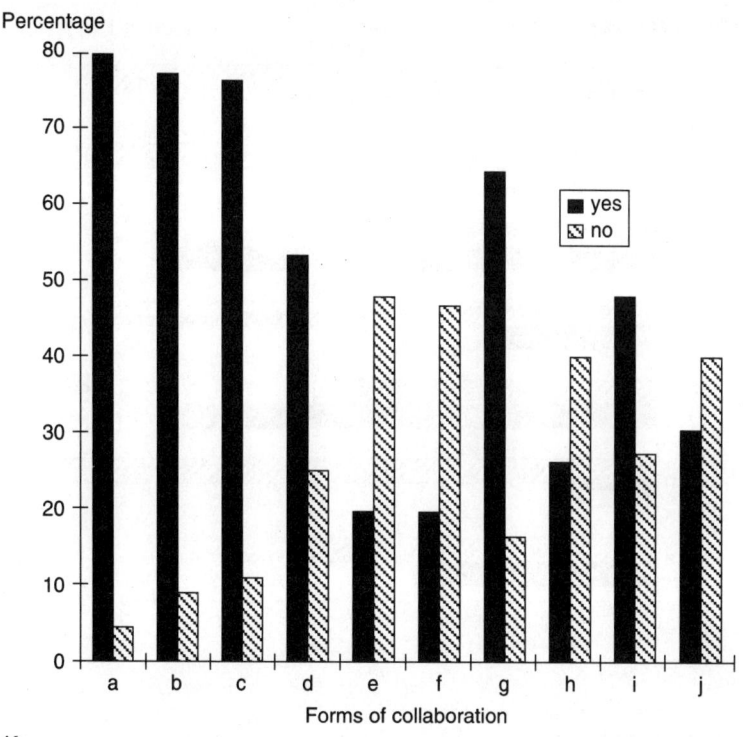

Collaboration for special needs: a national survey 31

Percentage

■ yes
▨ no

Forms of collaboration

Key:
a = exchanging information
b = planning joint special needs approaches and policies
c = undertaking joint special needs INSET activities
d = making the specialist expertise of teachers in one school available to teachers in other schools on a consultative/advisory basis
e = enabling teachers from one school to work directly with SEN pupils in another school
f = enabling pupils with SEN to spend some or all of their time in another school
g = exchanging SEN resources between schools
h = jointly managing finances, personnel, resources or facilities for special needs
i = negotiating jointly with the LEA and its services and/or with other service-providers in respect of special needs
j = formulating joint bids to funding bodies

Figure 2.2 Types of collaboration among schools

also involved themselves in sharing SEN resources or some level of teacher consultancy and advice. It was, however, much rarer for schools to share or exchange teaching staff, to teach each other's pupils or to manage joint funds.

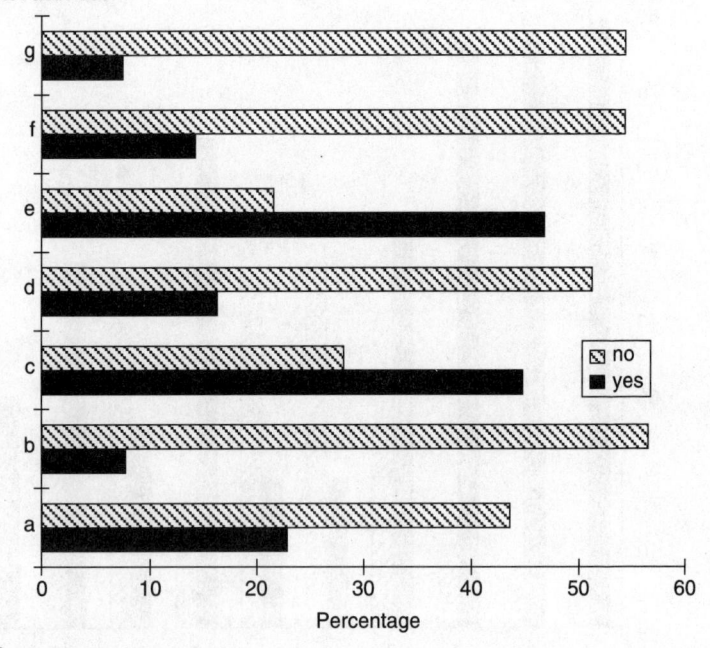

Cluster activities

Figure 2.3 Cluster activities for pupils with special educational needs

Key:
a = an agreed joint special needs policy
b = shared SENCO
c = operates agreed assessment and referral procedures
d = developed a pattern of coordinated SN provision across participating schools
e = agreed working arrangements with LEA services
f = established its own support services
g = established some other form of special needs provision

Figure 2.3 shows the sorts of provision for pupils with special educational needs which had resulted from these forms of collaboration. It was most common for participating schools to have developed agreed assessment and referral procedures (often in response to the demands of the Code of Practice) and/or to have negotiated agreed working arrangements with LEA services – usually the SEN support service or schools psychological service. In the latter case, these arrangements often (though not invariably) came about because the service played a key part in facilitating the cluster. One cluster, for instance, had, on its own initiative, persuaded its LEA SEN support service to provide schools with 'blocks' of support time on a rotational basis rather than with small weekly amounts of time. This, it claimed, had enabled it to shift the focus of support teachers' work from the tuition of individual pupils towards consultancy and joint planning with the schools' own teachers.

It was somewhat more unusual for schools to have coordinated their SEN provision in more comprehensive ways – by, for instance, appointing joint staff, designating a cluster special educational needs coordinator (SENCO) or developing a range of specialisms across participating schools. Nevertheless, such activities were not unheard of. One cluster, for instance, comprised four small primary schools the SEN budgets of which were too small to enable them to buy into the LEA/SEN support service to any effective extent. By working collaboratively, however, they were able – with the active encouragement of the LEA – to buy the time of a member of the support service to act as a sort of 'cluster coordinator', planning SEN provision across all four schools. Hence, they had been able to develop a common SEN policy, coordinate information-exchange across the school's own SENCOs and build up a shared resource base, in addition to negotiating an appropriate pattern of provision from the support service.

The range of clusters' collaborative activities is considerable. Nevertheless, there are two ways of imposing order on this diversity. First, it is possible to arrange clusters' activities along a continuum in terms of the extent to which they involve individual schools in surrendering more or less of their autonomy. Activities such as occasional meetings to exchange information or the development of agreed assessment and record-keeping procedures demand relatively few resources and have relatively little impact on participating schools. However, other activities – the appointment of shared staff, or the coordination of provision across schools, for instance – require participating schools both to invest considerable resource in the cluster and to surrender some of their rights to autonomous decision making. Looked at in this way, we find that the activities which are most commonly represented in our survey are those which involve the least surrender of autonomy. While this may be an artefact of our sampling strategy, it also accords with what one would intuitively expect and indicates that many – though by no means all – clusters are actually relatively loose confederations of schools which in most respects continue to go about their work independently.

Second, it is possible to categorize the activities undertaken by clusters in terms of their underlying purposes. Indeed, a few respondents were able to make these purposes explicit, perhaps by producing a cluster 'mission statement'. Even where this was not the case, however, it was possible to deduce underlying purposes by examining the range of activities undertaken by particular clusters. Although these purposes varied considerably, Table 2.1 attempts to summarize them into a series of categories and present some examples of each.

The list in Table 2.1 is almost certainly not exhaustive and the purposes shown here are, of course, not mutually exclusive. Nevertheless, these purposes can, as before, be arranged along a continuum according to the degree to which they require individual schools to surrender autonomy to the cluster: the provision of mutual support, for instance, scarcely impinges on the internal management of the school, while the joint management of resources or the creation of some system of representation requires that the cluster take on much more of a life of its own at the expense of the autonomy enjoyed by its constituent schools.

Beyond this, however, it is also evident that different purposes call for different forms of clustering. For instance, some of these purposes (such as the first two in Table 2.1) can be achieved without sophisticated management structures; others are likely to call for formal meetings, management committees, written constitutions and so on. Similarly, some purposes are entirely within-school matters which do not necessarily require involvement from the LEA, while others are crucially dependent on external involvement and may, indeed, need to be LEA-led.

The notion of a 'continuum' of levels of clustering, therefore, needs to be set alongside this typology of clustering purposes. It is certainly true that some clusters work together more closely than others. However, this may not be because they are more 'genuine' clusters or have 'progressed' into a more integrated form; it may simply be that they serve fundamentally different purposes which call for different structures and practices. We need, therefore, to be very cautious about assuming that we know what clusters 'should' look like, since clusters serving different purposes may take on very different forms; indeed, as we saw

Table 2.1 A typology of cluster purposes

Purpose	Example
The provision of mutual support to school staff	Regular meetings of SENCOs to discuss issues of common concern; associations of staff in 'low-incidence' special schools.
The coordination and development of policy and practice across schools	Pyramid clusters where common record-keeping procedures are developed or where joint approaches to literacy are formulated; clusters focusing on the development of IEP or SEN policy formats in response to the Code; clusters organizing their own INSET programmes.
The exchange of expertise	Clusters based on special schools, specially resourced schools or pyramids where specialist teachers from one school offer consultancy to teachers in other cluster schools.
The management of resources	LEA-initiated clusters managing their own devolved budgets; school-initiated clusters managing pooled resources to achieve economies of scale; clusters with enhanced resourcing offering a specialist service to schools and pupils in a wider area.
The creation of a focus for external services	Clusters negotiating special arrangements with LEA services; clusters acting as the 'base' for health or social services personnel
The enhancement of resources	Clusters bidding for funds outside the LEA (e.g. to TECs, the EU, ALBSU)
The establishment of a means of representation or negotiation	Clusters seeking representation on LEA working groups and negotiating with the LEA on behalf of cluster members

earlier, some forms of legitimate collaboration may not look like clustering at all. This caveat is important both for researchers, who can easily be seduced by the more high-profile forms of clustering, and, even more importantly, for educational managers and administrators, who might be tempted to determine the form of a cluster without reference to its purposes.

THE RESOURCING OF CLUSTERS

The types of collaboration among schools are inevitably linked to the question of resourcing. We know, for instance, that occasional and informal collaboration is quite possible within schools' existing resources and without any pooling of those resources; the exchange of information between schools in a pyramid when pupils transfer from one to the other is a common example of this. Similarly, we know that LEAs such as Nottinghamshire have established elaborate systems for delegating resources to clusters as such, and that these resources have to be managed through formal systems (Cade and Caffyn 1995). In our survey, well over half of respondents reported that their clusters had access to human or material resources, while over 40 per cent said they had access to financial resources. These resources were somewhat more likely to be provided by the schools themselves than directly by their LEAs.

A variety of patterns emerged where resources were provided by participating schools themselves. Some clusters operated a subscription system whereby individual schools made over relatively small amounts of funding to the cluster. This subscription might be on a flat rate (£30 in one case; £1000 in another) or in accordance with some sort of weighting system reflecting the LEA's LMS formula. Others operated more informally, with individual schools donating the time of their staff to undertake tasks on behalf of the cluster without any very tight accounting system. However, the pooling of resources within a cluster need not be on an 'equal shares' basis. Over a quarter of respondents, for instance, reported that human and material resources were provided by some schools within the cluster rather than others, while over 10 per cent said that one or other schools actually made funding available to their partners. While most of these examples consisted of schools (such as special schools) sharing additional resources which had been provided for that purpose by their LEAs, there were a few cases of schools acting out of a sort of enlightened self-interest to donate resources to their partners. Secondary schools, in particular, might see it as being in their interests to enable their feeder primaries to undertake early intervention. Similarly, there were a few clusters which had managed to secure funding from sources other than their LEA – the local TEC, for instance – and which were thus operating to some extent as autonomous organizations rather than as loose confederations. Indeed, one cluster reported that it had been established first and foremost as a means of generating income from such sources.

CLUSTER MANAGEMENT

The pattern of cluster management reflects closely that which we have seen in terms of resource management and the determination of the cluster's focus. In the large majority of cases, clusters were managed jointly by all participating schools, sometimes in partnership with the LEA. Only in very few cases (less than 10 per cent) was the management of the cluster seen as primarily a LEA responsibility. However, there were other patterns. Some clusters, for instance, reported that management was the responsibility of one or other participating schools. In some cases, this was because a special school or resourced mainstream school was taking the lead in offering services to its partners; in many others, however, this seemed to be simply a duty undertaken by one school (perhaps on a rotational basis) in order to facilitate the working of the cluster rather than a sign that the 'managing' school in any sense 'owned' the cluster.

Many clusters operated on a somewhat informal basis. Typically, headteachers and/or SENCOs met together more or less regularly to exchange information and plan future activities, with individuals chairing meetings and undertaking tasks on behalf of the cluster as the need arose. However, this was not always the case. Just under half of the respondents claimed that their clusters had some sort of formal management structure and, in a few cases, this included the designation of a cluster manager and the formulation of a cluster constitution. Frequently, these more formal arrangements were serviced by the LEA which provided a cluster manager (an educational psychologist or member of the SEN support service, perhaps) and a set of procedures. However, some clusters had developed these arrangements for themselves. One large cluster (28 schools), for instance, had an elaborate management mechanism, comprising: a programme of monthly meetings governed by a fixed agenda and culminating in an annual general meeting; a 'democratic' decision-making system in which each school had voting rights; a system of sub-groups

(Key Stage, Curriculum Support, Governor Support, SENCOs etc.) to undertake specific activities; a Steering Group to oversee the ongoing work of the cluster; a full-time cluster manager; and, an agreed system of funding by weighted subscription from each participating school.

CLUSTER TYPES

We have suggested above that there is some relationship between the purposes which clusters pursue, the activities they undertake and the management and resourcing structures they develop. This begs the question as to whether these features regularly cohere into distinct 'types' of clusters. Given the non-representative nature of the sample and the great diversity in the clusters which responded, our answer has to be somewhat tentative. Nevertheless, there do seem to be some broad differences between what we might call 'high-collaborating' and 'low-collaborating' clusters.

Most clusters, as we have seen, tend to be relatively small, to engage in joint activities which involve minimal surrender of autonomy and to be managed on a more-or-less informal basis. However, there are other clusters which are more far-reaching in their activities and which operate much more as cohesive organizations in their own right. Size appears to be a factor in this since, in large clusters, the numbers of schools involved necessitate more formal structures and generate a level of resource which makes more ambitious plans possible. However, there is also a tendency for longer-established clusters (those more than five years old) to work together more closely than their younger counterparts, to have developed more formal management structures, and to have access to their own resources. What we do not know, of course, is whether the longevity of the cluster makes possible the high level of collaboration, or whether the high level of collaboration ensures the cluster's longevity.

We know from the literature that many high-collaborating clusters originate in LEA initiatives and – as in, say, Devon, Nottinghamshire and Oxfordshire – reflecting both LEA policy and ongoing LEA support (at least prior to local government reorganization). However, we also know that not every cluster collaborates as closely as its LEA might wish, and our survey indicates that 'bottom-up' clusters are equally likely to generate high levels of collaboration. It may well be, therefore, that the issue of ownership and the sense that participating schools have that the cluster serves some real purpose is more important than the origin of the cluster or its place within LEA policy.

There are, then, certain tendencies within our sample for particular features to be found together. However, these tendencies do not quite amount to distinct cluster 'types'. This is partly because our sample contains a large number of exceptions to our proposed typology – young or small clusters which are very high collaborators, for instance. It is also because, as we have argued above, clusters can serve a wide range of purposes, take on a wide range of forms and engage in a multiplicity of activities. In common with Lunt *et al.* (1994), we found that 'each cluster arrangement was both unique, and very complex and dependent on very specific local circumstances and personnel' (p. 41). It may be, we suggest, more helpful to characterize clusters in terms of where they lie on a series of dimensions than it is to allocate them to a limited number of fixed 'types'.

IMPLICATIONS

It is worth reminding readers that our survey was concerned with something between a 'purposive' sample – clusters identified as having something interesting to tell us; and an 'opportunity' sample – clusters which 'happened' to volunteer themselves to take part. It has not sought to secure or analyse a representative sample of clusters across the country and cannot claim to be painting a national picture of clustering activities. Nevertheless, there do seem to be some important implications from our findings.

THE NATURE OF CLUSTERING

We have argued throughout this chapter that we should adopt a very broad view of what constitutes a 'cluster group'. The groups which responded to us were extremely diverse in form, operation and purpose. Insofar as they could be arranged on a continuum, it is certainly true that high-collaborating clusters constitute a form of educational organization which is significantly different both from the 'autonomous' school and from the 'centralized' LEA. However, the large numbers of low-collaborating clusters did not undertake such very different activities from those which most supposedly autonomous schools might be expected to undertake. All (or very nearly all) schools exchange information about pupils with other schools, coordinate (to some extent) their recording-keeping, harmonize their curricular provision, work together under the aegis of the LEA – and so on. Some schools may regard themselves as forming part of a 'cluster' as such, but this distinction is relatively unimportant in the face of the widespread nature of school collaboration.

The notion of a distinct phenomenon called 'the cluster' is misleading in another respect. One dimension along which clusters can be placed is the extent to which their collaboration is narrowly or widely focused. Where clusters have a narrow focus, it seems evident that participating schools must also be collaborating with other schools over a wide range of issues which are not within the cluster's remit. While the SENCO, for instance, is working with partner schools to develop a common format for Individual Education Plans (IEPs), the head of maths may be working with a different group of schools on curriculum development, the head of sixth form with different schools again in a post-16 consortium, the headteacher with a joint LEA-headteacher working group on funding – and so on. Where clusters have a wide focus, this multi-layered pattern of cooperation is clearly reflected in the complex structures which are set up to manage it.

The implication of this is that we need to see all schools as involved in complex patterns of collaboration. Some of these patterns are formalized through explicit clustering arrangements, and such arrangements may well create different conditions which facilitate collaboration. However, a simple dichotomy between highly formalized clusters on the one hand and autonomous schools on the other does not match the complexity of what actually happens between and among schools.

THE EXTENT OF CLUSTERING

This blurring of the boundaries between clusters and autonomous schools has implications for what we currently take to be the extent of clustering. Our survey, we have suggested, provides evidence that clustering is relatively widespread, in terms of the numbers of clusters responding to our inquiries, the certainty that there are many other clusters which did not respond and the indication that recent policy changes have given an impetus to clustering. However, if the distinction between less formal types of clustering and the sorts of collaboration in which very many schools are engaged is not particularly hard and fast, then we have to accept that, in a very real sense, clustering is an almost universal phenomenon.

This is not a purely academic argument. The policies of successive governments in recent years have sought to emphasize the autonomy of the individual school at the expense of the centralized control of the LEA. If, however, this is a false dichotomy, then policy might begin to build on a somewhat different image of the school – not as an unfettered and self-seeking organization maximizing its advantage in the education marketplace, but, as others have suggested (Goddard and Clinton 1994; Gallacher 1995), as part of a complex network of educational partnerships. The policy task then becomes less one of increasing the effectiveness of individual institutions and more one of managing the network as a whole so that provision is of a consistently high standard.

IMPLICATIONS FOR POLICY AND PRACTICE

This issue brings us to the implications or our findings for policy and practice in respect of inter-school collaboration. We address our comments in particular to teachers and LEA personnel who are considering whether and how to become involved in clustering activities.

Fitness for purpose

An implication of the diversity of clustering arrangements which we discovered is that there is no 'ideal' or 'right' way to cluster. Clusters come in all different shapes and sizes, serve all sorts of purposes, undertake all manner of activities, and are managed in all sorts of ways. Despite our efforts to impose some sort of order on this diversity, there is, in the final analysis, no simple continuum or typology from which blueprints for cluster development can be derived. We suggest, therefore, that those who manage or promote clusters need to audit their current and intended practices and structures and, in particular, to have a clear sense of how they relate to the underlying purpose which the cluster is intended to serve. The continua and typologies which we have suggested in this chapter are not intended to be definitive, but we hope they will provide useful starting points for such audits.

Catalysing developments

School and LEA personnel who are responsible for developing clusters may also need to consider what will act as the catalyst for that development. It is clear from many of the responses to our survey that clusters had not simply materialized out of nothing – and certainly not simply out of good intentions. Almost invariably when respondents told us something of the history of their clusters, they identified something which had acted as a catalyst. In broad terms, these catalysts fell into four types:

- a pre-existing grouping or other structure on the basis of which the cluster could develop (such as a TVEI consortium or a school pyramid);
- a human catalyst in the form of an energetic headteacher or LEA support service member;
- facilitation in the form of LEA pump-priming funds or administrative support;
- a need experienced by participants, such as the pressures placed on schools by the introduction of the Code of Practice or a change in LEA policy.

These catalysts might be present to different degrees in different clusters, but our findings seem to suggest that some level of catalysis will always be necessary for clusters to emerge.

Top-down or bottom-up?

Our survey does not enable us to answer definitively the question of whether top-down (i.e. LEA-initiated) or bottom-up (i.e. school-initiated) clusters are likely to be more effective and enduring. However, we can say with some certainty that the clusters which responded to our survey were almost invariably characterized by a relatively high level of autonomy and low level of LEA control. Moreover, many of them commented with some pride on 'their' practices, policies and achievements. The implication would seem to be that, although the LEA may have an important role to play in catalysing and facilitating clusters, some autonomy needs to be left to the clusters themselves so that they can take control of their own destinies and establish some degree of ownership over the collaborative process.

It should be acknowledged at this point that the autonomy of the cluster – like the autonomy of the school – can easily come to be in conflict with the necessity of the LEA's establishing some measure of control over special educational provision in its area. Indeed, there is a potential – and sometimes actual – conflict between some schools' views of clusters as a means of resisting LEA control, and some LEAs' views of clusters as a means of exerting precisely that control over 'maverick' headteachers. Some of the clusters in our survey were both very large and very powerful, operating almost like mini-LEAs. Such clusters effectively become quangos – unaccountable to anyone, yet challenging the authority both of their LEAs and (to a lesser extent) of the governing bodies of participating schools. Indeed, we encountered cases where particularly active clusters were influencing LEA policy to the disadvantage of schools which were outside the cluster framework.

This is perhaps a fitting issue with which to leave the reader. At the time of writing, the UK Government has made a series of proposals – for Education Action Zones, for special schools operating as centres of excellence, for specialist mainstream schools offering services to other schools in their locality – which mark a far greater commitment to the notion of clustering than has hitherto been evident at national level. At the same time, the continuing fragmentation of local authorities into smaller 'unitary' authorities, the proposals to give regional government offices a role in planning special needs provision and an overall tightening of central government control over the education system raise fresh questions about the future role of local education authorities. Our survey shows that collaboration between schools is by no means so rare as might be supposed and offers considerable potential for the efficient and effective delivery of educational services to pupils with special educational needs. The question that will shortly have to be answered, however, is whether the informal and diverse forms of collaboration reported here are to be encouraged to develop under the aegis of the LEA, or whether a more radical policy of establishing formally constituted clusters under the aegis of regional authorities is to emerge as an alternative strategy for managing the education system. If the latter is indeed to be the case, much can be learned from the 'natural experiments' currently taking place, but the issue of democratic control and accountability will need to be addressed urgently.

3

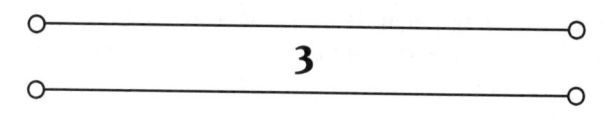

COLLABORATION IN ACTION

INTRODUCTION

The previous chapter provided an overview of the range of collaborative schemes currently operating in England and Wales. The amount of collaboration and its duration may seem surprising, given the explicit emphasis on competition in government policy over the last decade. However, its presence demonstrates that, in many areas, despite pressures to do the opposite, schools have found it beneficial to collaborate over a range of activities. This chapter will describe, in some detail, five examples of collaboration to support special educational needs which we studied as part of a research project.

THE RESEARCH

We have been interested for some time in the potential of collaboration between groups of schools to enhance the capability of schools to meet a wider range of special educational needs, and have now undertaken two substantial research projects to look at the operation of such collaborative arrangements, which we have called 'clusters'. For the purposes of the research, we have defined a cluster as follows:

> a relatively stable and long-term commitment among a group of schools to share some resources and decision-making about an area of school activity. There is a degree of formality, in that there are regular meetings of cluster schools to plan and

monitor the activity concerned. There is some commitment of resource (e.g. teacher time) and some loss of autonomy implied, since schools will have to negotiate some decisions about this area of activity. Clusters can be single phase (i.e. or primary or all secondary) or multi-phase, including special schools. They can include outside agencies, such as a health authority or local employers' organization. Their origins can be 'top-down' (i.e. LEA initiated) or 'bottom-up' (initiated by the schools themselves).

Clusters differ from networks, in that the former are more formal and well-defined systems. They also differ from 'federations' in that the latter imply the grouping of schools under one head teacher, and therefore a greater degree of loss of autonomy (Benford 1988).

In practice, the variations we have found in collaborative arrangements have led us to be somewhat less prescriptive about the formality and longevity of clusters. As the preceding chapter has demonstrated, there is a huge range of activity that can be characterized as 'collaborative', and which may or may not develop into a relatively stable and long-term relationship. We have also found that some relatively long-term clusters of schools have had difficulty in sustaining their commitment due to outside pressures, such as problems with funding, or the movement of key people. However, for the purposes of choosing 'clusters' of schools for detailed study, we tried to pick those which most nearly fitted our definition.

We undertook our first study in the early 1990s, as Local Management of Schools was being introduced. In that study, which is reported in Lunt *et al.* 1994, we focused on four examples of cluster activity in four different LEAs. We looked at the way the clusters had been set up, how they were currently operating and what were the perceived advantages and disadvantages for schools in being in a cluster grouping. In the later study, which took place when LMS was well-established and schools were more used to coping with the changes imposed by the National Curriculum and the new assessment arrangements, we studied a further five collaborative groupings of schools in five LEAs, widely dispersed throughout England. In each grouping, we interviewed the head teacher and SENCO in each school, the chair of governors or the special needs governor, and LEA support staff for special needs, including the psychological service. We also collected any documentation relating to the operation of the group, such as policy documents, formal agreements and minutes of meetings.

The findings from these five case studies will be discussed in some detail in this chapter. The five collaborative groups were chosen to reflect distinctive contexts, purposes, histories and patterns of activity. They will be briefly introduced below, and then discussed in more detail and some broad conclusions drawn from the findings about each group.

1 The Valley

This group of schools describes itself as a 'pyramid'. It consists of a secondary school and four primary schools in a remote rural area. The origins of the cluster lay in the realization of the head of the secondary school that the viability of his school depended on the viability of the four small primary schools which fed into it. This realization came before the 1988 Act had set up a competitive market for schools, but at a time when small rural schools were in danger of closing for economic reasons. The schools share a number of resources across many areas of the curriculum. They also jointly fund a special needs coordinator.

2 Wattford

This group was set up by the LEA as part of its attempts to allocate special education resources more equitably. The LEA was concerned about a high level of statement production which was leading to resources being tied very closely to individual pupils and leaving very little funding available to support less serious special needs in mainstream schools. The LEA decided to devolve funding for moderate learning difficulties to the level of 'families' of schools and to leave the decisions about which pupils should receive funding to a group of heads and SEN advisory and support professionals. The 'family' consists of one secondary and six primary schools in a semi-rural area. The secondary school and three of the primary schools are in the town and the three remaining primary schools are in the adjacent countryside.

3 Black Horse

This group was focused on a small country town. The 'partnership' is long-standing (i.e. pre-1988) and is part of a strategy promoted across the authority to encourage cooperation between primary and secondary schools in a number of the small country towns in the LEA as well as between groups of schools in its main city. Many initiatives from the LEA have been focused on partnership activities. The partnership studied consists of the secondary school and nine feeder primary schools.

4 Weston

This group, called an 'academic council', is located on the edge of a city in a large shire county. The suburb consists of a range of private and council housing, merging into the countryside. There are ten schools in the cluster – two secondary, seven primary and one special school. Each school in the cluster has a teacher with SENCO responsibilities and there is a joint appointment across the cluster of a SENCO to serve all the schools.

5 Woodside

This group is a large consortium of primary and secondary schools in an inner city area. The area is racially and ethnically mixed and socially deprived. The aim of the consortium was to raise the profile of the schools in the area, and to try to improve the image of the area generally. However, the huge problems of social deprivation and special needs confronting the schools made a focus on this aspect of the schools a key feature of the collaborative efforts.

COLLABORATING TO SURVIVE – ENHANCING PROVISION IN A RURAL AREA

The Valley cluster is located in a remote and hilly rural area, on the western edge of a largely rural county. It consists of a small secondary school (the high school) and its four feeder primary schools serving small villages and the surrounding farms. Collaboration between the schools started in 1983, mainly through concern about the survival of the small schools. The secondary school has about 220 pupils in the 11–16 age range, and the primary schools have between 40 and 90 pupils. The primary schools have teaching headteachers and very small staff numbers. Pupils from the primary schools predominantly move up to the secondary school, from which pupils then transfer to the sixth form college in the neighbouring market town.

The initiative for collaboration was first started when a new headteacher was appointed to the high school, although a degree of interaction between the schools already existed before this. With the encouragement of the senior county inspector, the headteachers began to meet, and this led to a resolve to share resources and to provide mutual curriculum support in the schools. The first resource to be shared was the high school's minibus, which opened up new possibilities for the primary schools, such as starting joint curricular activities for pupils in similar age groups. All the primary schools had mixed-age groupings (some had only two classes). Later, when the minibus needed replacing, the PTAs arranged a successful joint fund-raising event. The LEA, which valued this collaborative initiative, was persuaded to offer the schools 1.5 full-time equivalent (fte) of specialist staff for music, PE and special needs to serve the pupils of all the participating schools.

The schools set up a joint administrative framework. The group of headteachers meets monthly, under the chairmanship of the high school headteacher (the only full-time, non-teaching headteacher), and his school also provides the secretarial support. Decisions are reached by 'round-table' discussion, and the individual headteachers consult their staff about drawing up agendas. In addition, there are half-termly meetings of the primary headteachers and the infant and junior teachers (which also involve the heads as teachers). The chairs of the governing bodies of the schools initially met termly, and there were also some joint meetings of the PTAs. When new headteachers are appointed to the schools, a positive attitude towards cluster collaboration is one of the points taken into consideration.

When LMS was introduced, the schools switched to pooling portions of their funding to cover the joint activities. The LEA initially used its 'initiatives fund' to provide some support for the collaboration between schools. Over the years, this additional funding has been reduced, and the schools now have only their LMS allocations to fund their shared resources. The LEA includes an element in its pupil-based formula for special needs which is the same for all schools, but the LEA adds a small additional allowance for any pupils on free school meals and for any pupils who have statements. There is also a small further allowance for the annual review of pupils' statements.

The shared special needs provision mainly takes the form of a joint appointment of a SENCO to serve all the schools. The SENCO is nominally on the staff of the largest primary school, and has a permanent appointment with a variable time allocation. Each school funds the appointment in proportion to the time it requires for supporting its own pupils. Having a joint post enabled the schools to appoint a SENCO of a calibre none of them could have afforded on their own.

The current SENCO is the former headteacher of a county school for pupils with emotional and behaviour problems. She works with pupils in each of the schools at all stages of the Code of Practice, and when the Code was introduced, she drafted the special needs policies of the schools. The SENCO keeps the special needs registers for the schools in consultation with the teachers and deals with the paper work for any pupils being proposed for a Statement. At Stage 3 of the Code, she liaises with the county support services, and with the educational psychology service when any pupil is considered for a statutory assessment. The SENCO provides in-service training for teachers and learning support assistants, and also takes part in the in-service training programme for the governors of the schools.

The benefit of this collaboration for pupils is that the SENCO can provide support for teachers in all the schools, from the earliest stages of concern. Because she works across the phases, the SENCO can offer the security of continuity of support for the pupils. Parents appreciate this consistency of support for their children and for themselves. The SENCO's support for the teachers and the learning support assistants is grounded in her familiarity with the circumstances of the schools and their settings. This also gives teachers confidence in the SENCO's moderating judgements about the children's special educational needs. The headteachers appreciate the SENCO's contribution, since they would never have the time to deal with all the arrangements and paperwork.

There is, of course, a risk in a joint appointment arrangement such as this, that the schools, for their part, and the LEA for its, might leave the SENCO to take over responsibility for meeting all the special needs of the pupils. With regard to the schools, the risk is moderated by the scale of the SENCO's task, so that she inevitably has to work through the teachers as well. Her involvement in schools' special needs policies and the administrative aspects of the Code enable her to have an opportunity to influence the schools as a whole. With regard to the LEA, over recent years, the support staff have been reduced to such an extent for all schools, that the SENCO, in fact, is able to provide an invaluable supplement to what the LEA offers. Clearly in a SENCO post such as this, much depends on the quality of the person appointed and the trust they engender. Schools need to be confident that the SENCO serves them all equally.

COLLABORATING TO SUPPORT INCLUSION – DEVOLVING RESPONSIBILITY TO A 'FAMILY' OF SCHOOLS

Wattford is a group of seven schools, based in a small town of a large county authority. It was originally set up by the LEA as a 'family' of schools (the comprehensive and its six feeder primary schools) serving a geographical catchment area for the purpose of National Curriculum training and dissemination. The authority has actively encouraged this form of collaboration by providing resources for schools to work together. Of the seven schools in this 'family', three primary schools are rural, while three primary schools and the comprehensive school are in the town. The comprehensive school has about 700 pupils; the six primary schools range in size from 90 to 225 pupils.

The group works together at several levels. At a general level, the headteachers of the seven schools meet termly at the comprehensive school. There are also a number of collaborative activities, including an information leaflet, some common policies among the primary schools, collaboration over transition, and a number of informal contacts between staff. However, we will focus here on the group's collaboration in the field of SEN. This involves the same seven schools and their SENCOs. The SEN activity of the group originated in 1990/1, following the introduction of an LEA policy for SEN which aimed to integrate more children with moderate learning difficulties into mainstream schools; this policy was launched in 1990. The introduction of the LEA policy led to the headteachers of the Wattford family putting SEN on their agenda for the group and to SENCOs from five of the schools attending a course together.

As part of its policy on integration, in 1990 the LEA created eight 'area support groups' to coordinate resources for support in the mainstream at a local level. These were to operate as a kind of panel meeting to evaluate bids for additional resources (and needs) and to allocate resources across the schools in the groups. The way in which these funds are accessed is described in some detail in Chapter 5. If agreed, the resources (hours of support assistant) are allocated to the family of schools, for use by the individual school for the individual child, but organized and monitored at the level of the family. At the time of the study, there were six permanent support assistants assigned to this particular area support group, to be shared across the different families of schools according to need.

Wattford was also able to bid for development funds – for INSET, supply cover for INSET, topping up support assistant hours where the group agreed and where there was felt to be a need. These funds were placed in an account at the school of the headteacher who convenes Wattford family, and who also managed its finances. This permitted flexibility and a contingency fund for the schools.

The group is managed by the seven SENCOs, and convened by one of them who is both a headteacher and SENCO while another SENCO acts as secretary. In two of the six primary schools, the headteacher and SENCO are the same person; in the other four, there is a separate SENCO. Also centrally involved is the local EP who serves the group of schools and a SEN support teacher who spends time in all seven schools. They meet formally once a term; however, informally, there is much more contact, in particular between the six primary schools where frequent telephone calls serve to develop and maintain the network and the commitment to collaboration; for example, pupils with SEN are referred to as 'our' children, meaning Wattford group's children.

In the schools of the family, several of the headteachers had been in post for ten or more years, giving stability and continuity of personnel, and commitment to the group. SENCOs changed more frequently, several having gained promotion over the recent period. Overall, there appeared to be sufficient stability of staffing which contributed to sustain the ethos and commitment to the group collaboration. Wattford is organized, convened and led by one headteacher SENCO, who gives a lot of time and enthusiasm to it. The primary schools have a great commitment to collaboration, and feel that this works well for them. However, with the growth of parental choice, an increasing number of parents from the primary schools of the group choose not to send their children to the secondary school, despite it being the school designated by the LEA.

The family provides a context for developing a common understanding and definition of exceptionality, and a form of moderation across schools. It also provides a forum for supporting schools – the family may agree that one school has a particular (greater) need and so top up the allocation made by the area support group. They have developed a common format for recording children's needs, and are in the process of developing common assessment formats.

The Wattford family shares two special needs support teachers and some equipment which is kept at one school, and is available to the others. They arrange joint INSET and use some of their joint resources to pay for supply cover. During the visit, we became aware that the schools knew about each other's pupils with special needs, and were very 'considerate' towards each other, and aware of the relativity of need, and indeed were ready to support with advice, experience and even worksheets where one school had previous experience which could inform another's current difficulty. This had led to a shared understanding of SEN and a commitment to share resources and expertise.

The members of Wattford family considered that there were considerable benefits from their collaboration. They felt that pupils benefited from the increased expertise and confidence of the SENCO, and the fact that the teachers felt supported. In addition, there was the potential to share information about children with SEN with the school to which they are moving (usually the secondary school, though occasionally local transfer), and the opportunity to build links between teachers, and share expertise. In addition, it was possible to benefit from economies of scale by sharing the costs of training, and by sharing some equipment. Thus, they considered it to be 'more economical to pool together'. In Wattford, the group coordinator has an enormous commitment to collaboration and sharing, and is considered to be a driving force and a great help.

At the time of the research, there was a strong commitment to collaboration, in particular among the six primary schools, although there was some awareness that imminent budget cuts might make this more difficult. However, the majority of those interviewed had confidence, at the time, that the collaboration would survive and would continue in strength and activity. Even in the face of budget constraints, which might mean that it would be more difficult to release SENCOs to meet, there was a feeling of commitment and confidence in the collaboration, at least among primary schools.

PARTNERSHIPS AS POLICY – LEA-SUPPORTED COLLABORATION

The LEA in which the Black Horse group of schools is located has been developing the idea of partnerships between schools since the mid-1980s. Currently there are 31 partnerships operating in the LEA, six based on the city and the rest located around the small country towns and larger villages in the county. The original impetus for partnerships was to promote more effective liaison between primary and secondary schools over the transfer of pupils. However, more recent developments in partnership activities have focused on achievement, behaviour and discipline and a variety of INSET activities. The LEA has set up a 'Partnership Development Fund' which supports, on a matched funding basis, a variety of professional and curriculum development activities across groups of schools and phases. The availability of this funding (which is subject to bids from partnerships) has encouraged more formal organizational structures to emerge so that the partnership meetings are minuted, there is an agreed chair for meetings, etc.

The Black Horse partnership is centred on a small town in the south-west corner of the LEA. It consists of one mixed 11–18 comprehensive school of 1800 pupils (based in the town) and 15 primary schools, four of which are in the town and the remainder in outlying villages. There is also a special (SLD) school which plays some part in partnership activities. There is a complicated network of involvement of teachers as governors in schools, with many teachers being parent or community governors in schools other than their own. This level of involvement in local schools makes the links between schools especially close and may partly account for the robustness of the partnership.

The Black Horse partnership has been in existence since 1980 as a loose federation and was originally set up to ensure a smooth transition of pupils from primary to secondary school. More recently, the organizational structure has become more formalized and a formal agreement setting out the parameters of cooperation was signed by all the schools in 1992. This agreement stated that all the schools in the partnership were committed to close collaboration and cooperation and that the aims of the partnership were: to maintain and enhance the educational provision for all children in the schools; to share and develop good practice; to establish a common framework of policies; to make the best use of resources across the partnership; and, to identify and develop new opportunities within the partnership. Since 1992, the range of people involved in the partnership meetings and working groups has expanded to include teachers and governors, as well as heads and it has been involved in a number of initiatives, including the provision of a resource centre and the joint funding of a special needs advisory teacher.

The partnership has a steering committee which consists of three primary headteachers and the vice-principal of the secondary school. This committee decides how much of the joint funding for the partnership will go to each of the three groups responsible for different areas of activity: the special needs management group; the INSET group; and, the management group for the resource centre which is based in one of the primary schools. There are two ways in which partnership activities are funded: £3 per child on roll in each school is donated to pay for administrative costs, supply cover, conferences, etc.; and, funding from the schools' delegated SEN budgets is pooled to pay for the special needs advisory teacher. All money paid into the partnership by the schools for partnership activities is matched by the LEA. Thus, of £20,000 budgeted in 1996, half was paid by the LEA and half by the group of schools. This matched funding by the LEA has been a key stimulus for the development of the partnership in its current form. Currently, the partnership pays for 0.5 fte for the special needs advisory teacher, whose time is shared among the primary schools. The secondary school contributes to the salary, but does not use the teacher. The resource centre has a range of special needs resources which can be accessed by all the schools.

The benefits of the partnership, as perceived by those involved, are numerous. First, having a special needs advisory teacher who works across all the schools acts as a moderating influence when assessing the level of need. Second, the partnership promotes cooperation, rather than competition, between schools. For example, the four primary schools in the town explicitly encourage parents to visit their nearest school before making any choice about where to send their child. Third, the smaller schools can afford to buy in expertise, which they otherwise could not. Fourth, the class teachers can benefit from shared INSET across the schools and classroom assistants can also receive joint training. Fifth, matched funding from the LEA enhances the provision that can be made and the fact that the secondary school contributes a large share, but does not draw on the resources is also a help to the primary schools. The SENCOs in each school meet regularly and this reduces their sense of isolation. They are also in contact by telephone. Overall, collaboration has enhanced the educational provision available for all children, including those with special educational needs by improving teachers' confidence and expertise and by providing a broad forum for discussing and finding solutions to problems.

Although no disadvantages in collaboration were found by the partnership schools, there were some factors which made collaboration difficult. The major one was finding the time to attend the meetings which were required to enable the partnership to function. Another was the increasing squeeze on resources by the LEA, which made it difficult for some schools to pay their dues into the partnership. Two of the smaller schools had decided to forgo the benefits of additional help with SEN and access to the resource centre in order to save money. However, the head of the secondary school was optimistic that the partnership would continue because the benefits outweighed the difficulties.

A SHARED APPROACH TO SPECIAL NEEDS – PROVIDING A SEAMLESS WEB OF SUPPORT

The schools in Weston are located in a suburb on the edge of a provincial city. The seven primary and two comprehensive schools serve the population of a council estate and private housing merging into the countryside. A special school for around 80 pupils with severe learning difficulties is also located within the area, and is linked with the cluster. The seven primary schools have around 250 to 350 pupils, and the secondary schools have 900 and 1400 pupils respectively. The LEA is a large one, made up of several divisions.

Collaboration between the schools started around 1987. The LEA had a policy of encouraging schools in geographical areas to share in curriculum development, and to set up collaborative clusters for this purpose. As part of the in-service programme to support this development, the schools in this particular cluster set up a shared course in special needs for the headteachers and SENCOs in their schools, and this was encouraged by the local LEA officer responsible for special needs. The coordinated special needs provision arose within the curriculum development cluster arrangements.

The headteachers managing the cluster appoint one of their primary heads in turn to be responsible for the arrangements for pupils with special educational needs. The primary headteachers set up a special needs resource centre, housing materials and equipment, which also provides a base for meetings of the schools' SENCOs and of learning support assistants, and for meetings with the parents of pupils with specific learning difficulties. The special school makes its hydrotherapy pool and its computer-assisted learning equipment available to the other schools. Pupils from the mainstream schools come to the special school to help in supporting pupils in the special school, and a variety of joint activities take place.

The LEA's funding arrangements for special needs are built around the cluster school arrangements, since this enables the LEA to target the requirements of the individual schools more flexibly by delegating some funding decisions to the clusters. Each year, the clusters submit their special needs development plans and budgets. The funding of the individual primary schools is allocated on a historical basis, and a separate small amount is allocated to the cluster on the basis of a proxy index derived from the number of pupils taking free school meals. The special and secondary schools are individually funded for special needs – the secondary schools on a free-school-meals proxy index. The budget for pupils with statements is allocated on an individual statemented pupil and school basis by an LEA resource panel.

At the time of our study, 46 per cent of the available budget was devolved to clusters. At this time, the funding arrangements were also being reviewed through consultation with the clusters of schools in the LEA. The criteria by which the LEA evaluated the clusters' budget plans included the sharing of resources (including staff), the level of cooperation to meet pupils' special educational needs and the built-in flexibility, and the extent to which the allocation of funds within one cluster was carried out on an objective basis.

The schools in the Weston cluster used their budget to set up three joint posts: a 0.6 fte post for a Cluster SENCO to support all the schools; a part-time teacher to support pupils at transition from primary to secondary school; and, a 0.1 fte teacher to help pupils with specific learning difficulties. Plans were also being mooted for a teacher post to support pre-school pupils with special educational needs.

The role of the cluster SENCO is to act both as a specialist resource for the cluster of schools, and as an administrator for the special needs provision answerable to the headteacher responsible for special needs. She manages the special needs budget and runs the resources centre. She uses this as her base for in-service training, particularly for the learning support assistants. The cluster SENCO is responsible for the learning support assistants appointed for pupils with statements and she supports the part-timetabled SENCOs in the primary schools and the SENCOs in the secondary schools. She maintains the procedures for the Code of Practice for schools, preparing statements and reviewing pupils with statements.

The part-time teacher supporting pupils across the transition from primary to secondary school works with pupils and their parents, and her funding is shared between the primary and the secondary schools. The part-time teacher for children with specific learning difficulties provides individual support for pupils and their parents.

Ownership of responsibility for meeting pupils' special educational needs is clearly a striking feature of the schools in this cluster. The jointly appointed SENCO provides readily accessible expertise for all the schools. Both parents and children appreciate the level of concern shown and the consistency of the quality of support available. The shared special needs resources are valued by teachers, and their confidence in meeting pupils' special educational needs is raised through the advice and consultation which the cluster SENCO is able to offer. The headteachers can be assured that they are observing the requirements of the Code of Practice and that the cluster SENCO is maintaining the standard of provision.

The LEA strongly approves of the cluster arrangement, since, as mentioned above, it is able to delegate a significant part of its special needs responsibility to the clusters. The School Psychological Service supports the cluster arrangements by allocating a psychologist to serve the cluster. This greatly increases the usefulness of advice and support which the psychologist can give, since it allows him to become familiar with the support available in the cluster schools.

A CONSORTIUM TO RAISE EXPECTATIONS IN THE INNER CITY

Woodside is a deprived area in the inner city. The 1990 census showed that it had one of highest rates of unemployment in Britain, one of the highest rates of mobility and among the poorest housing stock. These factors provide a considerable challenge for the schools in the consortium, which consists of 16 primary schools, two secondary schools, a tertiary college, two nursery schools, a hospital school and a behaviour unit. The city council has recently been engaged in a huge programme of urban regeneration which has led to the building of a convention centre and indoor exhibition space and the refurbishment of public spaces in one part of the area. Thus, currently, there is a juxtaposition of material prosperity and commercial activity alongside severe deprivation and unemployment which provides both a challenge and an opportunity to the community, the schools and the commercial enterprises in the area.

Schools in the city are grouped into three districts, which are further divided into consortia loosely based on electoral districts (wards). These consortia are used by the LEA as administrative units for some aspects of its work. The Woodside consortium is more active than many others in the city in setting its own agenda and working to improve opportunities for the children in its schools. The heads meet as a consortium group once a term. They have appointed a chair, a secretary and a treasurer. Each school contributes 40p per child on roll to cover the administrative costs. The major aim of the heads is to raise the profile and improve the image of the local area. For example, they have produced a number of publications celebrating the area and its history and the achievements of the children in its schools. They have held conferences with high-profile speakers, such as Mary Warnock.

An abiding concern of the consortium is the level of special educational needs to be found in its schools. Research carried out by one of the headteachers as part of a Masters dissertation found that teachers in the schools identified 45 per cent of the pupils in the primary schools as having special educational needs. Of these, 14 per cent had severe problems which could not be dealt with within the normal classroom. This led to the setting up by the consortium of a working party to discuss ways in which the problem could be tackled on a consortium-wide basis, as they felt that the support from the LEA was not sufficient. They devised a scheme for training volunteers to work on a one-to-one basis with children in the classroom. Funding for the scheme was given through an inner-city regeneration grant. Other initiatives included consortium-wide training for teachers and classroom assistants in behaviour management and training of SENCOs.

Future plans include the setting up of a 'centre for learning' which would provide assessment and support for pupils with learning and behaviour difficulties and their parents. Staff from the Centre would also offer support and advice to classroom teachers. It could also be a base for psychologists and other support professionals such as speech therapists.

The consortium currently provides mutual support and generates new approaches to special needs in schools under a great deal of pressure. It has reduced isolation and enabled teachers to share both problems and solutions. The hospital school has played a key role in networking across the schools and providing advice and support. The heads have supported each other in times when one or other of them has been under public scrutiny. Cooperation, rather than competition, has become the *modus operandi* of the schools in this highly deprived area.

COMMON THEMES

This chapter and the previous one have attempted to describe some of the wide range of activities which groups of collaborating schools have undertaken to enhance their provision for pupils with special educational needs. In contrast to the common perception, fostered by the education reforms of the 1980s and 1990s, that relationships between schools are characterized by competition and fragmentation, we have discovered that there is a wide range of collaborative activity taking place – of which those working in and with schools must be well aware. However, the potential of collaboration is probably under-realized in many cases, and our detailed case studies give some idea of the ways in which schools working together can increase the level of expertise and resources available and empower schools to make significant improvements to the education of all their pupils, from the most to the least able. Thus, schools can become more inclusive in their approach to the children in their communities.

Some of the common themes which have emerged from our case studies are:

Concerns with transition

The catalyst for setting up clusters or groupings of schools is often a concern about pupils making a smooth transition from primary to secondary school. This is, of course, especially crucial for pupils with special educational needs. In two of the areas we studied, there was only one secondary school available, but in the other three clusters, pupils had a choice of two or more schools, and therefore close involvement with a group of primary schools gave the added benefit for the secondary schools of getting the pupils and their parents familiar with the school before the choices were made. Nevertheless, the experience in the Wattford grouping seems to indicate that being part of a cluster will not always reverse the opinion of parents about a less popular school.

LEA support

In three of the five case studies (Wattford, Black Horse and Weston), the LEA had a specific policy of encouraging cluster activity and gave extra funding to schools for that purpose. In the Valley, the LEA had been impressed by the benefits of the cluster and had provided funding for shared staff appointments. In Woodside, there was no specific funding to encourage cluster activity around special educational needs, but the heads of the consortium schools were hoping to put pressure on the LEA to provide it.

Increased teacher confidence

All the case study schools reported increased confidence on the part of teachers, and particularly SENCOs, in providing for pupils with special educational needs. In part, this was due to cross-cluster in-service training (which also included classroom assistants), and, in part, due to the sense that schools were not working in isolation; that they were facing the same problems.

Economies of scale

Many of the smaller primary schools benefited from being part of a cluster as this gave them the opportunity to share funding of teaching staff and other resources. In particular, the joint SENCO appointment in the Valley meant that four small primary schools with teaching heads could afford to buy in help with the procedures of the Code of Practice, as well as expertise in the classroom management of special educational needs, which individually they could not have afforded.

Access to expertise

This was a bonus for all the schools, since they could share the funding of specialist teachers and advisers and could ensure that outside professionals working in the schools were familiar with the needs of all the schools in the cluster and would work with schools on a shared basis.

Enhanced resourcing

This was a key factor, particularly in recent times, when education budgets have been constrained and LEA funding has been cut. For clusters where the LEA matched funding (Black Horse) or devolved funding to the cluster (Wattford), there was an obvious incentive to continue to collaborate (even though two of the Black Horse schools had withdrawn for financial reasons). In some clusters the secondary school made a financial contribution, but did not draw on the resources, thus effectively subsidizing special educational provision in the primary schools.

More inclusive educational provision

This was an explicit aim of LEA policy in the area in which the Wattford 'family' was located. It was not explicit in other cases, but the result of enhanced capability and resourcing was a greater willingness in the cluster schools to keep children with quite severe difficulties in the mainstream.

Parity of esteem

Part of the aim of the clusters was to reduce the harmful effects of competition and the creation of 'sink' schools. Not all schools were equally popular in the cluster groups; nevertheless, the careful management of the transition from primary to secondary school meant that discrepancies between schools were minimized. Heads acted as supports to one another and did not indulge in aggressive 'marketing' of their schools.

Shared responsibility

Those involved in the management of clusters, usually the heads and/or the SENCOs, felt a responsibility for providing a high standard of education for all the children in their community, and especially for those with special educational needs. This sharing meant that children with special educational needs were not seen as a burden to be passed on to another institution or 'expert', but as members of the school to be provided for by the school, supported by the cluster.

Moderating effect

Children with special needs and the resources required to support them were discussed and decisions were made at the level of the cluster, rather than the individual school. This process had a moderating effect, and led to shared understandings about levels of need and the level of appropriate resources to meet needs.

Parental satisfaction

Schools reported that parents were highly satisfied by the continuity and consistency of support their children were being given.

CONCLUSION

This chapter and the preceding one have illustrated some of the wide range of collaborative groupings which currently exist in the English school system. Despite the difficulties and pressures which beset schools, it can be seen that the potential of collaboration to increase the efficiency and effectiveness of support for pupils with special educational needs is being used by these groups of schools, with beneficial results, both for teacher morale and parental satisfaction. The following chapter will discuss the ways in which collaborations are set up and maintained, which factors appear to support and which hinder the maintenance of cooperation between groups of schools.

4

THE ORGANIZATION AND MANAGEMENT OF COLLABORATION

This chapter will discuss the ways in which collaborative activity is organized and managed, and the phenomenon of the continuing existence of both formal and informal collaboration in the British education system that has been subject to reorganization into a 'quasi-market' (LeGrand and Bartlett 1993) which, as discussed in Chapter 1, was supposed to deliver the Government's goals of a system characterized by 'efficiency, effectiveness and economy' (Audit Commission 1988).

Such reorganizations are not peculiar to the British system; they have taken place in a number of other Western developed countries, including Australia, New Zealand and the USA. Other European education systems, many of which have been characterized by extreme centralization and bureaucratization, have also been decentralized. The main thrust of these reforms is to replace existing bureaucratic, centrally managed education systems with decentralized 'site-based' systems, where the responsibility for the delivery and the quality of education is located at the school level (Lawton 1992).

Thompson *et al.* (1991) suggest that there are three main ways to coordinate social systems: markets, hierarchies and networks. Hierarchies (i.e. bureaucracies) are rule-bound, unresponsive and de-skilling. However, the rules in which they operate provide some safeguards against unfairness. This was the dominant organizational form in the British education system pre-1988. Markets are flexible, quick to respond and customer-driven. The quasi-market in education was set up to emulate these features. However, markets favour the most advantaged and do not concern themselves with equity, and are therefore problematic as an organizing principle for welfare services such as education (LeGrand and Bartlett 1993). Networks can be more or less formal sub-groups which can operate within markets and bureaucracies. They can protect the interests of their members and can generate personal commitment because of their interactive nature.

All of these organizational forms are present in the current system of special educational provision. The statement procedure (and the Code of Practice) are archetypal bureaucratic mechanisms and suffer from many of the problems which stem from this type of organization. They are formal, slow and relatively inflexible. They generate large amounts of paperwork and the decision-making process is cumbersome and remote. Parents feel disadvantaged when caught up in such systems, as is well known from research into the statutory assessment procedures (e.g. Goacher *et al.* 1988), and professionals are often frustrated because they feel that their autonomy is compromised by bureaucratic constraints on their decision-making responsibilities. Nevertheless, bureaucratic systems provide some safeguards for children and parents (e.g. the appeal mechanisms). They also locate the accountability for the provision of a good service closer to those who make decisions about policy and resourcing. The current decentralized system has tended to focus attention on accountability at the school rather than the political or administrative level.

Markets are flexible, quick to react and responsive to their customers. Schools operating in the current system of choice are part of a local market and have to respond to this fact. Therefore they face dilemmas about meeting the needs of more problematic children because some of their customers may not want to use schools which have large numbers of such children. The most effective schools will be able to operate inclusively and meet the needs of all their pupils. Nevertheless, such a response is easier to maintain if the competition for pupils created by the market system is less intense. One way of accomplishing this is for schools to collaborate in the ways in which we have described in the previous two chapters; that is, to create collaborative networks.

Although the 1988 and 1993 Education Acts have attempted to replace hierarchies (or bureaucracies) by markets, networks appear to be an enduring form of coordination which operates through micro-politics (Ball 1987) and which exist both in bureaucratic and in market systems. Strategies to beat the market (or to mitigate its effects) are a feature of both commercial and public sector markets. Networks also operate to bypass or influence the perceived inflexibility of hierarchical bureaucracies. Powell (1991: 271–2) characterizes networks as:

> complex: they involve neither the specific criteria of the market, nor the familiar paternalism of the hierarchy. A basic assumption of network relationships is that one party is dependent on resources controlled by another, and that there are gains to be had by pooling resources. In essence, the parties to the network agree to forgo the right to pursue their own interests at the expense of others.

He suggests that networks operate when there is a need for efficient and reliable information. The price mechanism of the market gives poor information, dependent, as it is, on hearsay and reputation. The information flows within bureaucracies are slow, because they are controlled by set procedures and rules. He contends that networks are especially useful for the exchange of commodities whose value is not easily measured (such as expertise, or high-quality special needs support). The benefits which respondents in our clusters reported included: the ability to employ high calibre staff; parental satisfaction; mutual support among the schools; increased influence over the LEA; and smooth transfer from primary to secondary school for pupils.

Thus, although some of the clusters we studied were set up within the LEA bureaucracies as part of their hierarchical system, they also operated as networks, and served, in some cases, to subvert bureaucratic control. More recently (post-1988), they have served to mitigate the effects of a local market among schools and acted to stabilize the educational environment for their communities. Our examples of collaborative networks at the more formalized end of the spectrum illustrate a response to the problems of bureaucracies and markets. They offer the opportunity for schools, as a cluster, to practise self-sufficiency in providing for special educational needs. They provide the environment in which schools can share resources and expertise, and can feel protected, to some extent, from the full rigours of competition. So, how can such arrangements be fostered? The next section draws on our research findings, and those from other studies of collaborative school networks, to discuss ways in which the benefits of collaboration can be supported and extended.

WHAT CAN COLLABORATING GROUPS OF SCHOOLS DO THAT INDIVIDUAL SCHOOLS AND LEAs CANNOT?

We have stressed the advantages of clusters for meeting a wider range of needs in schools and maximizing inclusive education. However, it must be acknowledged that some schools (particularly large primary and secondary schools and those with very few pupils with special educational needs) may feel that they can support all their pupils without the need to collaborate with others. Collaboration requires trust because it relies on informal or non-legal agreements to share resources and to open up to the scrutiny of others. Traditional, bureaucratic arrangements are bound by formal rules, which safeguard participants in their dealings with each other. Markets are underpinned by a notion that each participant will seek to maximize his or her position. Those being asked to collaborate in such circumstances are required to trust the other partners in the arrangement and to make a 'leap into faith' in circumstances which are fraught with anxiety and risk (Giddens 1991). Thus, the advantages of collaboration are not always obvious for individual schools, and the overall benefit may be at the level of the community, so entering into such voluntary arrangements can involve an element of altruism. For example, in the Black Horse partnership described in the previous chapter, the secondary school invested resources in the collaboration but did not draw on them. There was an indirect benefit to the school, in that children coming into the school from the primary schools would have benefited from the extra support at primary level, and the relationship between the primary schools and the secondary would have been strengthened by its active support for them. Thus, less tangible benefits may be the result of collaboration as well as the more direct ones described in Chapter 3.

WHAT IS THE BEST WAY TO SET UP AND MANAGE A CLUSTER? WHAT MAKES CLUSTER ARRANGEMENTS ROBUST?

From the research reported here, and earlier research on cluster arrangements, we have described a number of factors which support the setting up and continuation of collaborative arrangements. What follows is not a recipe, since every grouping will have its own ecology and history, but it makes some general points about setting up and running collaborations of this type.

We have discussed elsewhere (Lunt *et al.* 1994) whether 'bottom-up' or 'top-down' groupings are more likely to succeed and have concluded that LEA support is a crucial factor, but ownership by the group of schools is also very important. Our research found examples of successful clusters which originated from the schools themselves deciding to cooperate (bottom-up) and others where the impetus came from the LEA (top-down). The national survey reported in Chapter 2 indicates that the more active collaborative groups value their autonomy and might even challenge the LEA over some issues. However, the role of the LEA in promoting and supporting collaborative arrangements is a key factor in the 'value-added' which such groups can achieve, not least because LEAs are targeting extra resources to cluster groups to improve provision for pupils with learning needs.

The management of the group is a key issue and one which needs sensitive handling. Most of the groups we studied were managed by a committee, chaired in rotation by one of the participating headteachers, although some were chaired by a SENCO. The most important factor, however, was that the person managing the cluster had the trust of all participants. Some of the larger groups also had sub-groups which organized different aspects of the work of the group. The size of the grouping was not an important factor in predicting the dynamism or robustness of the cluster – some of the clusters in our study were small (four or five schools) and some much bigger (12 or more schools). What was more important was the sense of a cluster identity and a commitment to the community served by the group of schools.

There was often a catalyst or key issue which sparked the cluster into life – for example, the wish of the headteachers in Woodside to improve the image of their area, or the realization of the head of the secondary school in the Valley that the small village schools would be under threat if they did not receive support.

The major threat to the collaborations we studied was that of reductions in LEA support and resourcing. Although the benefits of the clusters were clear to all participants, as Levačić (1995) found, schools which are under real financial pressure have to practise economy, rather than efficiency or effectiveness, and therefore choose the cheapest option they can in order to save money in the short term. Thus, the real gains of collaboration, which, as already discussed, are often longer-term in their outcomes, may be dispensed with because of short-term crisis management. School budgets are set annually, and can fluctuate from year to year, so that longer-term planning is often difficult, and so the commitment to share resources is reviewed by schools on an annual basis, which sometimes puts the maintenance of collaboration under pressure.

HOW CAN A BALANCE BE STRUCK BETWEEN AUTONOMY AND COLLABORATION, SO THAT ALL PARTIES TO THE CLUSTER ARRANGEMENTS (INCLUDING GOVERNORS AND PARENTS) ARE SATISFIED?

This is an important issue for schools, since they have to be responsive to the views of parents and governors. The successful clusters we studied had the support of their governors, and as described in Chapter 3, there was a degree of cross-involvement in some clusters, with teachers in one school being governors in another. The loss of autonomy which accompanied involvement in the cluster was not seen as a negative aspect, as it was offset by the feeling of support and mutuality which was gained for heads, SENCOs and other staff. Collaboration was seen as a source of strength, and the enthusiasm for clusters communicated itself to governors and parents, insofar as they were aware of it.

WHAT INCENTIVES WILL MOTIVATE SCHOOLS TO COLLABORATE?

The main reason for the collaboration between schools is that it gives an opportunity for schools to enhance the provision they are able to make for their pupils. This may be because the LEA gives extra resources to cluster groups, or because small schools can use pooled resources to buy in expertise that they could not afford individually, or because communication between primary and secondary schools is improved, to the benefit of both. Thus there needs to be a 'pay off' of some kind in order for schools to put time and energy into collaboration and to consider the needs of other schools in the community, as well as those of their own school. As suggested above, it appears that competition can be destructive if taken to extremes, and the schools in our studies have decided that it is not in the interests of the pupils in their communities for one or two schools to prosper at the expense of others.

WHAT USEFUL ROLE CAN LEAs PLAY IN SUPPORTING CLUSTERS?

It seems to be important for LEAs to support and encourage, but not to force the pace of collaboration. The most successful clusters appear to be those who have already seen good reasons to collaborate in the interests of becoming more effective. LEAs can respond to this by providing financial incentives (for example, delegating funding for specific collaborative activities) or expertise (for example, using the local adviser to facilitate collaboration and give support to cluster activities designed to promote school improvement). The delegation of decision making about the allocation of funding for special needs support in mainstream appears to be a powerful way of ensuring a meaningful level of collaboration, as the example of Wattford demonstrates.

HOW SHOULD THE RELATIVE RESPONSIBILITIES OF SCHOOLS, CLUSTERS AND LEAs BE FORMULATED?

This is obviously a matter for negotiation, within the framework provided by legislation. The *Education Bill* (DfEE 1998) proposes an enhanced role for LEAs in monitoring standards and setting targets, in negotiation with schools. There will also be new benchmarking information which will allow schools to evaluate their performance relative to other similar schools. The schools in one cluster may not necessarily be similar in terms of intake and other factors used in bench-marking, but they can support each other to improve performance, where this is seen to be necessary.

Some LEAs (for example, Nottinghamshire and some parts of Wiltshire) already delegate significant funding and responsibility to local groups of schools. These schools, along with advisers and psychologists, make decisions about the allocation of resources to schools for the support of pupils with special educational needs. This demonstrates that it is possible for LEAs to decentralize, not only the delivery of services to a local group of schools, but also responsibility and decision making.

IS SHARING RESOURCES FOR SEN IN A CLUSTER MORE EFFICIENT AND ECONOMIC THAN INDIVIDUAL RESOURCING OF SCHOOLS AND PUPILS?

The allocation of resources to meet special educational needs is problematic, as has been acknowledged in Audit Commission reports and in the recent Green Paper on Special Education (DfEE 1997b). We have argued elsewhere in this book, that economies of scale can be achieved by schools sharing resources and by cluster groups being made responsible for the allocation of resources within the group. If allocation of resources in this way (i.e. through delegation to a cluster of schools) is also part of a strategy for reducing statement rates to around 1.5 per cent of the pupil population, this would result in significant savings, since the statement procedures themselves use up a large proportion of LEAs special needs budgets – funding which could otherwise be targeted towards provision. As the Green Paper acknowledges, the statement procedure has become a heavy burden for LEAs, and some means needs to be found to restrict the use of the procedures to those with severe and highly complex needs, which could not be met without significant extra resources for the support of the individual child. Currently, where statement rates are around 3–4 per cent of the pupil population, the procedures are being used for pupils with moderate learning and behaviour problems, which can be met in the mainstream with some allocation of extra resources. This, as has been demonstrated, could be decided upon by a SEN team at the cluster level, without all the paraphernalia and expense of statutory assessment.

Thus, it appears that clusters or other collaborative arrangements have the potential both to save money and to allow the more efficient use of resources at both the school and the LEA level.

WHAT BENEFITS ARE THERE FOR SCHOOL STAFF IN GENERAL FROM BEING IN A CLUSTER?

We have already rehearsed many of these in other chapters, but can summarize the benefits for staff (including support staff) as follows:

1 increased confidence in meeting pupils' needs;
2 more extensive training to meet needs;
3 extra resources available in the classroom;
4 more effective support from the SENCO and from SEN advisory staff;
5 reduction in feelings of isolation and being left to cope alone;
6 the opportunity to develop professional skills to meet a wide range of learning needs.

WHAT BENEFITS ARE THERE FOR SCHOOL MANAGEMENT (INCLUDING SENCOs) FROM BEING IN A CLUSTER?

In addition to those benefits listed above for all staff, heads and SENCOs were providing mutual support for each other. The access they had to other schools' advice and perceptions about SEN levels across a group of schools enabled them to have a more informed and balanced view about needs in their own school. For heads, the fostering of collegiality and a minimizing of competition between schools for resources were additional benefits. Being in a cluster seemed to mitigate the worst effects of competition between schools, for example, the dumping of problematic children in the least popular schools. Thus there was perceived to be a fairness in the way in which children whose needs were harder to meet were coped with across a group of schools.

ARE THERE ANY DISADVANTAGES FOR SCHOOLS FROM BEING IN A CLUSTER?

None of our respondents could think of any disadvantages. It was acknowledged that schools had to give up some of their autonomy in order to participate, but this was not seen as a problem. If the LEA was supportive, and did not use the existence of the cluster to cut back on resources, then the benefits would continue to outweigh the problem of the extra time that needed to be devoted to keeping the group in operation.

ARE THERE PROBLEMS OF ACCOUNTABILITY WITH CLUSTERS?

It has been suggested (see Chapter 2) that there could be problems with accountability if clusters became too powerful. They might challenge the role of the LEA and their use of resources might not be adequately monitored. Depending on the way they are set up, clusters are accountable: to the LEA for the use of funds devolved to them and to their individual governing bodies. It might be that some clusters would wish to set up a governors' committee with governors from every school represented, in order to be accountable for cluster decisions, but we did not come across any examples of such arrangements in our research. Schools are currently held accountable by governors and by the publication of test results and Ofsted reports. If both LEAs and schools are clear about the remit of the cluster and the extent of its powers, then there appear to be sufficient mechanisms to ensure accountability.

SHOULD A SYSTEM OF CLUSTERS BECOME A MORE FORMALIZED FEATURE OF SPECIAL EDUCATIONAL PROVISION?

Given the benefits described (more efficient and effective use of resources, a greater level of inclusion, the minimizing of the harmful effects of competition on the most vulnerable pupils, and the enhanced feelings of competence and capability among school staff) the question arises whether a system of collaborating groups of schools, such as those described in this book, should become a formalized feature of special educational provision.

The Government's stated aim in the Green Paper is to support a more inclusive education system. They also want to reduce the rate of statements and to make more efficient use of resources. The White Paper wants to see the effectiveness of schools enhanced and for educational standards to be raised. The evidence from our research is that collaboration between schools will help to achieve all these aims. As we argued in Chapter 1, the fragmentation of the school system and the pressures of competition have led to a situation where the rate of exclusions has risen sharply and where the statement rate remains high, despite the wish of LEAs and the Government to reduce it. The Green Paper focuses on collaboration as one way of achieving these aims and suggests that clusters of primary, secondary and special schools could act as mutual support and provide the necessary expertise to support more inclusive schools. These ideas will be developed further in the final chapter of this book.

5
RESOURCING ADDITIONAL NEEDS

INTRODUCTION

One of the greatest challenges for local authorities is how to distribute resources to meet pupils' special educational needs, allocate these equitably and target them effectively; a parallel challenge for schools is how to make effective use of their own SEN resources, and how to provide flexible and differentiated provision to meet the needs of the wide range of pupils in mainstream schools. These challenges occur in a context of finite resources and increased accountability.

Recent developments both in legislation and in the overall context of education in this country (see Chapter 1) have led to a growing gap between the level of response that schools can make to the diversity of pupils' needs through their own budgets, and the resources available through the statement procedure and provided by the LEA. Schools attempt to bridge this gap by putting pressure on the LEA for additional resources, using the only apparent means available, through statements. Thus there has been a considerable increase in numbers of pupils with statements, numbers of cases going to Tribunal, and numbers of pupils identified individually whom schools feel unable to support. In the light of increasing pressures on limited resources and financial constraints, there are clearly questions about where decisions about resources are made, the different levels of decision making in relation to SEN, and the different levels of responsibility for meeting pupils' SEN.

Following the 1988 Education Act, under LMS, the majority of the SEN budget has been delegated to schools which are then expected to make provision for all but a tiny minority of pupils from their delegated budget. The small minority of pupils with 'severe and complex' needs receive additional funding from the LEA through the statement procedure which is intended for about 2 per cent of all pupils. However, at the same time, LEA support services have been reduced because of the requirement on LEAs to delegate at least 90 per cent of the budget to schools, while the pressures of the National Curriculum and schools' league tables have meant that schools have become less able to focus or to spend resources on meeting SEN. It is reported that the special needs budget is currently £2.5 billion a year, which constitutes 12.5 per cent of schools' budgets (Barnard 1997).

Schools receive funding for SEN from different sources: school-based through age-weighted pupil units (AWPU) and the weighting for SEN; school-based through the LMS formula; and support for non-statemented SEN from LEA through support services (but this is dwindling). They are expected to meet the needs of almost all pupils from their delegated budgets. However, the allocation of resources for SEN at the school level through the formula has led to difficulties in targeting effectively, and to monitoring their use, particularly in the absence of any earmarking, and it is clear that the problem of 'resource drift' has meant that schools find it increasingly difficult to provide adequately for vulnerable pupils. As schools find themselves under financial pressures, funds 'intended' for SEN and allocated on the basis of the formula, using for example free school meals indicators, may be used for other equally 'pressing' purposes, since they cannot be earmarked and protected for a particular use. In this increasingly difficult context, and with pressures from parents of individual children and the threat of the Tribunal, schools have therefore resorted to seeking additional support through individual statements, thus creating a tension between the allocation of resources at the school level and at the level of the individual child.

Thus, as schools find it harder to meet the diversity of pupils' needs from their own resources, and as parents are more demanding and prepared to use litigation in pursuit of a share of scarce resources for their children, the number of statements has increased substantially in recent years. A survey for the DfEE by Coopers & Lybrand (1996) reported that the number of statements issued had risen by almost 40 per cent in five years, leading to 3 per cent of children with statements compared with the 2 per cent envisaged by the Warnock Committee in 1978 (DES 1978). Reduced LEA support services mean that schools have less help from the LEA and are left on their own to meet pupils' special needs. This, together with parental pressure and demand for resources, has led to a rise in demand for statements to a point where 3 per cent of children now have statements compared to the 2 per cent envisaged by the Warnock Report in 1978 (DfEE 1997b). In addition, appeals registered with the SEN Tribunal rose by half in its first two years to 1622 in 1995/6 (Barnard 1997). This occurs in a context (see Chapter 1) where external pressures on schools and on teachers have caused them to adopt pupil selection and financial policies which maximize their competitiveness, and where pupils with special educational needs are not attractive to schools unless they bring with them considerably enhanced resources.

It is worth reminding ourselves that some of the reasons for this have been inherent in the legislation since 1981. The Audit Commission/HMI report (1992a) identified some of the problems inherent in and resultant from the 1981 Act as: a lack of clarity about what constitutes SEN and about the respective responsibilities of the school and LEA; a lack of clear accountability by schools and LEAs for the progress made by pupils, and accountability by schools to the LEA for the resources they receive; and a lack of incentives for LEAs to implement the 1981 Act (Audit Commission/HMI 1992a and 1992b; Vevers 1992). The 1992 report was followed by a report in 1994 which identified progress since the 1992 report, but highlighted issues which still needed to be addressed by LEAs; these included 'ensuring schools are aware of the amount they receive for pupils with special needs through their normal allocation under formula funding' (Audit Commission 1994: 20). Although these difficulties were in part addressed by the changes under the 1993 Act, in particular its Code of Practice and new system of appeals under the Tribunal, the 1993 Act did not address the fundamental difficulties in the definition of special educational needs, nor some of the dilemmas and tensions inherent in the system of resourcing for SEN (Lunt and Evans 1994; Marsh 1995).

One of these dilemmas concerns the question whether to resource individual pupils or schools, and hence how to target resources for SEN. One approach commonly used by a large number of LEAs (Fletcher-Campbell 1996; Marsh 1997) is the use of 'proxy indicators', such as free school meals, based on the assumption that schools in disadvantaged areas (with more children with free school meals) will have more children with special educational needs (no correlation at the individual child level is being made). Another approach favoured more recently, has been the use of an SEN audit (in some cases now adopting the Code of Practice stages) to identify the numbers of pupils with different levels of need. This claims to identify individual pupils, but has the disadvantage of providing potentially perverse incentives and rewarding schools for identifying greater numbers of pupils, or of failing to 'add value' to pupils with SEN. This resource paradox (i.e. the tendency for the system to allocate more resources to schools who identify more 'failing' pupils) is one of the factors which may have led to the increase in demand for more resources for SEN. The Code of Practice (DfEE 1994a) appears to encourage an individual approach to the identification of pupils' SEN, and, as mentioned earlier, the 1996 Act re-affirms the definition of special educational needs provided by earlier legislation.

Marsh (1997) identifies the following eight principles for allocating resources: (i) responsiveness to needs; (ii) equity; (iii) effectiveness; (iv) accountability; (v) simplicity; (vi) stability of funding; (vii) efficiency and value for money; and, (viii) cost containment and need to reduce statementing. The first four of these may be seen as principles which are based mainly on ideals, while the last four may be perceived to be based mainly on expediency. Although it might be desirable to have a system based entirely on ideals, this needs to be combined with the realities and practicalities of financial planning and decision making within the constraints of the allocated budget. Although each of these principles on its own is likely to lead to a different system for allocating additional resources, the challenge is to devise a system which combines these principles as far as possible (see also Lee 1996). The Green Paper *Excellence for All Children* (DfEE 1997b) promotes an inclusive vision: among practical steps to promote inclusion one alternative is 'to seek ways of celebrating the success of those schools which improve their ability to provide for a wide range of special needs'; one way of celebrating this success would be through resourcing such success, and allocating resources at levels below stage 4 and the statement level, or allocating resources to schools which succeeded in reducing the numbers of pupils identified individually.

Although the intention of the 1981 Act was for statements to be used only for the tiny minority of pupils whose needs were 'severe and complex' (that is, those who would previously have been placed in special schools) it is well-known that they have been used as a means to gain additional resources for individual children with a wide range of difficulties in mainstream schools (see above). While this is to be welcomed as an indication that more pupils with severe and complex needs are being educated in mainstream schools, statements have also been used for a wider group of pupils who have been identified individually for individual resourcing.

The question of how many pupils to identify individually (1 per cent, 2 per cent, 18 per cent or 20 per cent) must be addressed at the level of the LEA or even nationally and is to some extent dependent on and closely related to the amount spent on education as a whole. Thus the *SEN Initiative* report recommended a single unified SEN budget, with a rational system for determining the overall budget and the numbers of pupils whose needs should be met. This would include a way of allocating resources at pre-statement level, avoiding perverse incentives and the use of statements to allocate resources (Coopers & Lybrand 1996).

The challenge to LEAs of resourcing for SEN has recently been increased both by the commitment to inclusion (DfEE 1997b; Thomas 1997; Thomas *et al.* 1997) and by the continued commitment to parental choice which entails the maintenance of both mainstream and special school systems to meet pupils' special educational needs. The Green Paper states that 'we want to look at ways of shifting resources from expensive remediation to cost-effective prevention and early intervention; to shift the emphasis from procedures to practical support' (DfEE 1997b). This chapter considers some ways in which this may be possible through schools collaborating.

DELEGATING RESOURCES TO A GROUP OF SCHOOLS

Recent legislation, in particular LMS, has reduced the capacity for LEAs to organize and provide support services for SEN. Yet individual schools may not be able to afford to provide the support or expertise needed by pupils on their roll. For this reason, groups of schools which have some formal links may provide a level between the LEA and the individual school, at which it may be possible to provide expertise and achieve some economies of scale. Some local authorities have developed an explicit policy to encourage collaboration between schools, and may make this a requirement for bids for funding. This occurs in the area of special needs as well as in other areas of schools' activity.

In one example studied, the local authority created a structure within its overall SEN policy to organize schools into groups, usually a secondary and its feeder primaries, and delegated most of the centrally retained resources for special needs to these groups of schools to manage through their local area management teams.

Thus, in the area we visited, resources (support teacher time, classroom assistant hours, money) were delegated to the group of seven schools, a secondary school and its feeder primaries. In this way, the group had its own resources, which operated in two ways, first through providing the salary for support assistants and second through providing development funds. In order to gain access to support assistants, individual schools made an application in respect of any individual children they considered to have 'exceptional' need. These applications were discussed at the group meeting of the SENCOs of the schools in the group; this acted as a form of moderation and helped to define 'exceptionality' in the group. Those agreed by the group meeting to constitute 'exceptional need' then went on to the local SEN panel to be considered for allocation of additional resources. The task of the panel was thus to evaluate the need for additional resources between the groups of schools, and again to serve a moderating function. The other way in which this group of schools had access to group resources was through bids for development funds, for example for INSET, for supply cover for INSET, or for topping up support assistant hours where the group of schools agreed that there was an additional need. These funds were placed in an account at the school of the convenor of the group, who also managed the finances of the group. This permitted some flexibility and a contingency fund for the group to use as it considered appropriate, and gave the group of schools responsibility for monitoring the level of need and the use of resources and enabled the authority to distinguish between predictable and unpredictable additional needs.

In another LEA, 46 per cent of the available budget for statements was devolved to the group of schools for joint decision-making on its allocation within the group of schools. This was intended to top up a school's existing resources to help the school to provide for children with special educational needs, and allocations were made according to an agreed formula which at the time took into account historical patterns of spending and numbers on roll.

Delegating funds for primary pupils with moderate learning difficulties was part of the strategy in another LEA to increase inclusion and to reduce the schools' dependence on statements as a means of gaining additional resources, as part of the 'local approach'. These resources were delegated to the groups of schools without the need for statements, thus saving administrative time and costs, and permitting whole-school planning rather than the coordination of individually allocated resources through statements.

MATCHED-FUNDING FOR COLLABORATION

Another way in which LEAs may encourage collaboration between schools was demonstrated by one LEA which requested schools to put in collaborative bids for additional resources and matched these from LEA funds. In this LEA, a group of schools pooled resources in two ways, first by contributing £3 per child on roll to pay for the administrative costs of organizing the group, supply cover and conferences for the group of schools, and secondly by pooling funds from the schools' delegated budgets to pay for a special needs advisory support teacher.

All the money paid into the collaborative group by the schools was matched by the LEA which had a strong commitment to collaboration between groups of schools and encouraged and rewarded this by matched-funding of collaborative initiatives. Under this scheme, the group of schools put in a collaborative bid for a programme of activities: in the year of the study, the bid was for £20,000 of which the LEA provided half while the other half was provided by the schools themselves. In this way, the authority was able to support collaboration between schools, which in turn were rewarded by the authority with funds for collaborative programmes and activities.

JOINT APPOINTMENTS TO A GROUP OF SCHOOLS

A very common way of schools collaborating over resources for SEN is through joint appointments of SENCOs, support teachers or support assistants. This has the advantage of achieving economies of scale and permitting the appointment of specialist posts, at the same time as providing a 'moderating' role which is achieved through working in several different schools over time. Several groups of schools in different LEAs had joint appointments of specialist posts, usually SENCOs, and in one case a behaviour support teacher. Other benefits from this kind of arrangement have included the sharing of equipment and expertise across the schools.

In one group of schools, there were several appointments made to the group of schools as a whole: a 0.6 fte SENCO, a part-time support teacher to support pupils at their transition between primary and secondary, and a 0.1 fte teacher support for specific learning difficulties. There are also joint appointments of three part-time assistants. These are regarded as group resources. The SENCO, for example, provides expert support for the SENCOs of the individual schools, and is responsible for the group special needs centre which is located in one of the primary schools. The centre houses shared materials and equipment, and provides the base for meetings for SENCOs and learning support assistants (LSAs), and for INSET.

Another LEA funded a SENCO for the group of five schools (a secondary and its four feeder primary schools); when LEA funding ended, the schools took over and funded the shared SENCO from their LMS delegated budget: the SENCO is jointly appointed and funded by the five schools, and provides expertise which none of the schools individually could afford. In a further LEA, a group of schools shared two special needs support teachers, funded by the LEA for the group, and working across the group of schools supporting individual pupils judged by the group to be in greatest need. This enabled the support teachers to develop and share expertise, as well as to exercise some form of moderating function across the schools in relation to levels of SEN.

A large group of 17 schools funded a special needs advisory support teacher (SNAST) from their delegated budgets. One of the perceived benefits was the SNAST overall view of special needs across the schools which had a moderating effect. Another perceived benefit was the ability of small schools to buy in a share of SNAST time. In another authority, the focus of the group of schools' collaboration was on pupils' behaviour and the joint appointment was a behaviour support teacher who coordinated a system of INSET and teacher exchange across the secondary schools in the group. A measurable outcome of this was a reduction in the number of referrals for behaviour support to the Educational Psychology Service, and a reduction in the number of statements in these schools.

Clearly, there are major benefits to be gained both for schools and for LEAs from joint appointments to meet pupils' SEN across the schools in the group. However, there were examples of other shared resources which may be more flexible and easier to coordinate in the current climate.

SHARED USE OF RESOURCES

The origins of one group's collaboration lay in their sharing resources for INSET. This group of schools, which consisted of ten schools, two comprehensives, seven primary and one special school, arranged for a course on special needs to be run for their staff at one of their primary schools. The group continues to hold one joint INSET day each year, as well as collaborating in other ways.

Another (rural) group of schools started their collaboration through sharing the High School minibus and computer equipment; this was followed by joint fund-raising which enabled them to buy a communal minibus for the group of schools, and which has persisted, enabling all schools to share a relatively expensive resource.

In another LEA, the group of schools raised their own funds for the administration of the group by contributing 40p per child on roll at each of the schools. These schools held annual high-profile conferences which have succeeded in providing a focus for special needs across the group of schools. At the time of the study, the group of schools was considering setting up a centre for learning, which they hoped would be part-funded by the LEA and part-funded from their delegated budgets. This centre would provide a base for part-time withdrawal of pupils for assessment and support, a resource centre for parents, while the staff of the centre would act as a resource for the group of schools and would go into the schools to offer advice and support to class teachers and SENCOs.

ADDITIONAL RESOURCING TO A SCHOOL IN THE GROUP

In another example, the LEA identified specific schools for additional resourcing in respect of a particular type of SEN. Thus additionally resourced schools received extra resources to act as a base for pupils with that type of disability (for example, physical impairment or moderate learning difficulties). In this way, pupils in the area covered by the group of schools with these SEN were expected to attend the Additionally Resourced School, which was able to meet their needs in mainstream provision. This enabled the LEA to achieve economies of scale, for example by adapting a mainstream primary school to meet the needs of physically disabled pupils; it facilitated planning since such needs would be relatively predictable; and it permitted greater inclusive provision across the authority. The Additionally Resourced School therefore served as the resource base or 'unit' for pupils with particular disabilities. Although this meant that parents of pupils with SEN were not given a choice of mainstream school, it did enable planning and efficient resourcing, and meant that pupils with significant SEN were able to be included in mainstream provision through a planned and explicit policy.

CONCLUSIONS

We have provided examples where groups of schools shared resources to meet the SEN of pupils in the area covered by the schools. These examples demonstrate that it is possible to delegate resources to the group of schools, and that this may increase community and local involvement and ownership, and that scarce resources may be enhanced through sharing. It would appear that there are benefits from these kind of arrangements both for schools and for LEAs. For schools there are benefits from sharing expertise, being able to afford more materials and equipment by sharing their use and economies of scale, and planning at the school level. For LEAs there are benefits in terms of groups of schools providing an intermediate level between the LEA and the individual schools, enabling moderation of SEN across a groups of schools, and facilitating planning of the allocation and targeting of additional resources across the LEA. In addition, there was some evidence that delegation of additional resources to groups of schools increased the schools' sense of ownership and responsibility.

The issue of shared resources raises again the question of collaboration between schools as a 'top-down' or a 'bottom-up' approach (see Lunt *et al.* 1994). The examples described show evidence of LEAs using the allocation or delegation of resources to a group of schools as part of an LEA strategy and policy in relation to good practice and/or provision for pupils with SEN. This is LEA-led and forms a 'top-down' initiative. However, as suggested (Lunt *et al.* 1994), collaboration works most effectively if 'top-down' initiatives are complemented by 'bottom-up' approaches, as for example shown in the example of matched-funding described above. Nevertheless, it was striking to observe a number of examples of genuine 'bottom-up' collaboration in which groups of schools were prepared to pool their resources in order to achieve a collaborative outcome.

Among the objectives both for schools and LEAs must be to make the most efficient and effective use of available resources, and to find the means of targeting these to those schools most in need. If resources are targeted to schools in this way, there needs to be a system for monitoring their use and their effectiveness. A further objective for LEAs must be to reduce the number of pupils who are identified individually to the very small group with 'severe and complex' needs (for example, the 1.75 per cent mentioned by Pijl and Meijer 1991), whose needs it is not possible to meet from schools' delegated resources; individual identification thus indicates exceptionality and the need for LEA support. However, a further goal then has to be to enhance the capacity of ordinary schools to meet a wide diversity of needs. This means planning the allocation and sharing of resources between schools and groups of schools to meet needs which are 'predictable' (see Gray and Dessent 1993), and which are agreed across the group of schools, thus confining the use of statements and individual identification to the small number of pupils with severe and unpredictable additional educational needs, indicating 'exceptionality', and beyond those 'generally available' in mainstream schools.

6

EFFECTIVE TEACHING AND LEARNING

Current thinking about ways of furthering effective teaching and learning for pupils with special educational needs is taking place in the context of two main issues in education – raising standards and promoting inclusive education. In this chapter, we look at the way that collaborating to meet pupils' special educational needs makes an impact on effective learning and teaching in the context of these two issues.

Concern to raise standards of achievement in schools is common in many countries at the present time. The source of this concern is ultimately the quest for economic competitiveness and economic growth, as we pointed out in the introductory chapter. This has been the concern which leads to international studies of education systems such as those carried out by the Centre for Educational Research and Innovation of the OECD (1995). The findings indicated that, in many countries, a significant proportion of pupils were found to be 'at risk' of failing in school, and that schools were not meeting their learning needs. The present Secretary of State responsible for education, David Blunkett, wrote in his introduction to the Government's White Paper on Education (DfEE 1997a): 'To overcome economic and social disadvantage and to make equality of opportunity a reality, we must strive to eliminate, and never excuse, underachievement in the most deprived parts of our country.'

The current flood of research into 'school effectiveness' and 'school improvement' has been an attempt to respond to some of these concerns. Earlier research had indicated that schools were not able to counter the effects of social disadvantage, but these findings have been questioned in these studies. They have looked to the quality of school and classroom management as the main determinant of pupil achievement (Creemers 1994; Hopkins and Harris 1997). Factors such as leadership styles were considered with regard to school management, and 'whole-class teaching' with regard to classroom management. The latter was specifically promoted as part of the 'back to basics' policies of the 1988 to 1996 period of the previous Government, which specifically promoted whole-class teaching. This notion was based on the claim that these approaches accounted for the alleged higher achievement of pupils in Pacific Rim countries.

More recently it has been reported (Sutcliffe 1997) that some of these countries are now dissatisfied with the outcomes of their educational approaches, and are planning to move towards smaller classes, less whole-class teaching, and to lessen competitive pressure on pupils. Researchers have also begun to question again how far a focus on raising standards of achievement in schools will itself counter the effect on pupils of social disadvantage (Dyson 1997). Nevertheless, the quest for ways to raise achievement goes on. For example, the present Government's National Literacy Strategy (DfEE 1997d) includes much advice on how schools can organize their teaching, so that the National Curriculum Level 4 target can be reached by 80 per cent of 11-year-olds by 2002.

The 80 per cent notion is significant in terms of our topic, since it raises the question about how the remaining 20 per cent of pupils can also be helped to make progress. As several commentators have mentioned (Norwich 1998), having a target for the '80 per cent' of pupils does not preclude targets for progress among the remaining pupils. As we mention in the introductory chapter, these are the pupils whose vulnerability may require a greater degree of flexibility from the teaching offered in schools. This flexibility of response is one of the challenges posed by the promotion of inclusive education in the present Government's Green Paper on special educational needs policies (DfEE 1997b). The extent of this challenge has been indicated by the rise, over recent years, in the demand for statements for pupils, and by the number of statements maintained by LEAs. Nichol (1997) reported that the number of statements had risen from 140,000 to 217,000 between 1990 and 1995. He points out that this increase cannot be afforded indefinitely. Furthermore, it does not represent an effective use of the available resources, and the Green Paper also concurs with this view.

In earlier chapters we have drawn attention to this 'gap' between the level of response which schools can make to the diversity of pupils' needs, and the support which schools are demanding for individual pupils through the statement procedure. The gap raises questions about how schools can become more effective and flexible in meeting their pupils' needs, and about how LEA and other support services can be more effective in helping schools and their pupils.

Inclusive education demands greater responsiveness from schools, so that they can be empowered towards closing this 'gap'. As we have pointed out in Chapter 4, collaborative groupings represent one way in which schools can take on a greater empowerment to this end. In this chapter, we describe some of the ways in which we found that collaboration enabled schools to increase their effectiveness and flexibility in responding to the diversity of their pupils' learning needs in general, and in their support of pupils with special educational needs in particular. In the next chapter, we will consider how collaboration can increase the support which services outside the school can offer schools.

It has become increasingly evident (Wedell 1995; Barber 1996; Meijer and Stevens 1997) that the way education systems are organized creates a degree of rigidity which hampers schools' capacity to respond to the diversity of their pupils' learning needs. In the UK, the financial constraints on schools have made the pressures to compete for pupil numbers more severe. Schools have been concerned about how to maintain their budgets, and this has often seemed to inhibit more creative approaches to education. For example, in such a climate, an impending Ofsted inspection might make a school more likely to conform to the 'official' exhortation to whole-class teaching. The concern would be, that Ofsted inspectors might make a negative report, which would then appear in the local press, and possibly damage the reputation of the school.

'Whole-class' teaching has been taken as an example, since it is well known that such an approach needs to be used judiciously to meet the demands both of the curriculum and of the learning needs of pupils. If this approach is used inappropriately, teachers face the problem described by Slavin (1987: 159)

> Perhaps the most difficult problem of class organisation is dealing with the fact that students come into the class with

different levels of knowledge, skills and learning rate and motivation. Teachers can always be sure that if they teach one lesson to a whole class, some students will learn more quickly than others. Some students may not learn the lesson at all.

In our introductory chapter, we pointed out that 'inclusion' requires schools to take on a much more flexible approach, based on the acknowledgement of the diversity of pupils. We currently have the paradox that schools are being encouraged to become more inclusive and to increase their responsiveness to pupils' learning needs, while aspects of the prevailing organizational patterns and policies militate against teachers' scope for responsiveness. As Wedell (1997: 152) points out:

> one is seeking the right for pupils with special educational needs to be included in educational environments which ... are predicated on misconceived assumptions about the homogeneity of pupils' learning needs.

Such a context tends schools and their teachers towards an 'integration' type of response. Pugach (1995: 16) in her survey of attempts at inclusive practice in the USA found such a tendency:

> although something new was definitely going on in these classrooms, they ... seemed to be operating on the same set of fundamental assumptions about teaching and learning that have characterized past practice in both special and general education.

Pugach goes on to list the assumptions made in these approaches:

1 that the basic curriculum philosophy in general education is acceptable,
2 that special education's role is the 'softening of the blow' of that curriculum ...
3 that practices ... provide an adequate buffer for the dilemmas posed by the standard curriculum paradigm and standard teaching practices.

So how can schools become more able to respond flexibly to the special educational needs of their pupils? As we have mentioned before, schools have to feel confident in order to be flexible in their approach – both in the implementation of the curriculum, and in matching the nature and level of support to the nature and degree of pupils' special educational needs. This 'matching' includes the support which pupils can gain from teachers' general level of responsiveness to pupil diversity, including the help which teachers can mobilize in the form of pupil peer support, parent participation and classroom assistant support. It also encompasses the more particular response which teachers can offer with the guidance of the school's special educational needs coordinator (SENCO), and beyond this with support from agencies outside the school, as indicated by the Code of Practice (DfEE 1994a).

Similarly, schools have to be confident in taking a comprehensive view of the curriculum:

> The prevailing focus on the limited subject-based conception of the National Curriculum itself impedes the scope to 'include' pupils with SENs. Teachers do much to support pupils' progress within the 'broad and balanced' conception of the curriculum, but this is insufficiently acknowledged and promoted within the current educational ethos.
> (SENCO-forum 1998)

Responsiveness to pupils' special educational needs requires that teachers have the opportunity to adopt a problem-solving approach (an approach which is also implicit in the successive stages of the Code of Practice). This involves teachers in successive cycles of attempting to understand a pupil's needs, choosing a teaching goal and an approach which matches the needs, evaluating whether pupils make progress, and then if necessary, modifying their approach. In order to be able to undertake such a problem-solving approach, teachers need a good understanding of the pupil, the pupil's learning needs and of the relevant aspects of the broad curriculum within which the pupil is expected to make progress. Such responsiveness makes considerable demands on teachers.

Ainscow (1993) describes the kind of school ethos and management that is needed to support teachers in such a problem-solving approach, and to achieve a flexible deployment of staffing and other help. He quotes Rosenholtz's distinction between 'stuck' and 'moving' schools (Rosenholtz 1989). Schools can be called 'stuck', when they have a well-established working structure, within which teachers have developed their own way of working, and are loth to risk altering it. 'Moving' schools, by contrast, are ones that seek to improve their responsiveness to their pupils, where teachers help each other, plan together, and share ideas and resources. As we describe below, collaboration between schools not only extends the scope for this kind of sharing beyond the individual school, but it also offers mutual encouragement to the schools within the current constraints mentioned above.

We found that there were a number of ways in which schools in collaborative groups were able to increase the flexibility of their response to their pupils' learning needs. Clearly, collaboration did not make the dilemma facing schools which we described above disappear, but as we showed in Chapter 2, collaboration occurred despite the fact that the 1988 to 1996 Education Acts promoted competition. At that time, one of the teachers in our study pointed out 'you would think that the legislation is actually designed to make it difficult for us to collaborate'.

COMPETITIVE PRESSURES

Collaboration automatically has the effect of relieving some of the competitive pressures. We found that, in some groupings there was a specific aim to avoid competition for pupils between schools. An example of this was an explicit agreement in one grouping that all heads would encourage parents, in the first instance, to consider sending their children to the school which was nearest to them. One grouping of schools drew up a 'Code of Practice for Admissions' which stated: 'parents . . . are advised to visit the school for the catchment area in which they live as a matter of course, before coming to any decision on choice of school'.

Such an agreement indicated the mutual respect between schools which grew out of their collaboration. Not surprisingly, such orientations also enabled all the schools to feel that each of them was willing to serve the range of needs occurring within their local pupil population. As a result, competition did not become a constraint on their efforts to meet the special educational needs of the pupils in their school.

SCHOOLS' SPECIAL EDUCATIONAL NEEDS POLICIES

It is well known that schools' policies may just be documents which are kept in filing cabinets to be brought out for inspections. On the other hand, the policies may be created through mutual discussion in school, and consequently can make an impact on practice. Special needs policies represent schools' preparedness to meet the diversity of their pupils' learning needs, and so can have a direct effect on teachers' day-to-day actions in the classroom. We found that collaboration between schools often included a shared approach to drawing up policies, which gave the policies status within schools. The policies tended to be a reflection of a school's wider concern with its pupils as individuals, including the intention to meet the diversity of pupils' learning needs, and to allocate funds and other resources to achieve this.

Those charged with the responsibility of drawing up the policies were able to share ideas with their colleagues in other schools, and this joint activity made it possible to achieve policies which were more relevant and supportive. The very fact that special educational needs featured as a substantive concern between collaborating schools made it likely that special needs policies were then used as a basis for practice, and would be kept 'live' through review in the light of experience. Consequently, teachers' response to pupils' needs started from a baseline of greater preparedness for flexibility.

FURTHER PROFESSIONAL DEVELOPMENT

A number of collaborative arrangements involved shared staff development – for teachers and also for Learning Support Assistants (LSAs). Schools chose common dates for staff development days, and then jointly planned activities and contributions from specialist speakers. As a result, the task of setting up the occasion was shared – as well as any cost of bringing in an expert from outside. In one grouping of schools, collaboration to meet pupils' special educational needs grew out of such a shared further professional development project.

Shared staff development provides an example of some of the conflicts which schools face in agreeing to collaborate. While the advantages mentioned above are obvious, individual schools may also be concerned that their own weaknesses and problems may become exposed to others. Needless to say, schools have found that the opposite occurs. They find that their individual problems are common to other schools. As a result they can capitalize on each other's experience in solving the problems. Two examples from our study illustrate this point.

In one grouping of schools, there was concern about managing behaviour difficulties in classes. The schools used their in-service funding to enable teachers to visit each other's schools to observe the classroom management approaches used by the teachers. This arrangement for observation was linked with joint in-service sessions where approaches to behaviour management were discussed among the participating teachers. All those taking part found this staff development of significant help, since they were able to examine the nature of successful, as well as unsuccessful, practice. The staff development opportunity greatly enhanced the teachers' capacity to implement positive behaviour approaches, and made much more effective use of the available in-service funds than any of the schools could have achieved on its own.

This example shows how a collaborative ethos enabled schools to open themselves up to observation and evaluation in a way which might otherwise be unlikely to occur.

The other example is also concerned with behaviour management, and involved an even closer interaction between schools. This occurred as part of the collaboration among secondary schools in a town which were concerned about the level of behaviour problems among their pupils. They decided to allocate a teacher for half-a-day-a-week to form a team to support pupils in each other's schools. The LEA responded by offering some time from its specialist support staff to provide in-service training for the teachers. The team was managed by the heads of the schools, with the advice of the specialist teacher.

Following their in-service training, the teachers were then allocated work for the allotted time in one of the schools other than their own, supporting pupils or teachers in their class, according to whatever was found most helpful by the school. This arrangement involved a high degree of trust between the participating schools, since their teachers would become very familiar with the problems of the schools to which they were allocated.

However, the very fact that the help was being given by class teachers made their support more acceptable to the teachers being helped, and the additional expertise the supporting teachers were offering then permeated to the other members of staff in the schools. Here again was an example where limited funds were being used in a way which multiplied the effectiveness of the investment.

SHARED RESOURCE BASES FOR MATERIALS AND EQUIPMENT

Some groupings of schools decided to set up joint resource bases for materials and equipment for helping pupils, as mentioned in Chapter 3. Teachers in schools invariably create or acquire materials, equipment and computer programs to help individual pupils or groups with particular learning difficulties. Under current financial constraints, it is increasingly difficult for schools to afford the range of items which would be helpful to the variety of pupils. At any one time, teachers in an individual school may have need for only some of the items, and so this situation offers scope for sharing. Obviously, the arrangement has to allow easy access to materials and equipment, and so resource bases should be set up in schools which are conveniently located. However, there are also other solutions. In the rural Valley grouping described in Chapter 3, schools use the school buses to send items from the base to the schools. Sharing materials and equipment clearly needs some organization, such as an index of what is available, and when. In a later section, we mention examples where this is arranged by SENCOs. Resource centres are also useful places for staff development, and in another grouping (Weston in Chapter 3) they were used for teachers and LSAs to meet to discuss approaches to meeting their pupils' special educational needs.

COLLABORATION BETWEEN SENCOs IN GROUPINGS OF SCHOOLS

There has been considerable concern that schools' SENCOs have received insufficient support to carry out their responsibilities under the Code of Practice. For example, Ofsted inspectors found that a significant proportion had not received specific training

(Ofsted 1996b). Some studies found that the level of pedagogical expertise which was demanded in the formulation of Individual Education Plans (IEPs) for pupils was a particular challenge to SENCOs (Dyson *et al.* 1997; Ofsted 1997). Most SENCOs find the procedural requirements of the Code, such as the documentation for IEPs, record-keeping and the form-filling for pupils moving to stage 4 of the statement process, very time-consuming – even when they have followed the advice issued by the DfEE (1997c). SENCOs have to work under considerable pressure, as Lewis and her colleagues found (Lewis *et al.* 1996). In 45 per cent of primary and 21 per cent of secondary schools, SENCOs had no time allocated to their duties. Furthermore, SENCOs, particularly those in primary schools, tend to feel somewhat isolated from professional support in their schools because, unlike subject specialists, they are frequently the only people with their particular responsibility.

In groupings of schools which collaborate to meet pupils' special educational needs, SENCOs have a context in which they can come together to support each other. In some groupings, meetings are specifically organized to provide such support (as we report below). However, there are also instances where, in neighbouring schools, SENCOs themselves took the initiative to come together for regular meetings at which they could discuss difficulties and problems arising in their work, in order to attempt to find some solutions from their combined experience. Jones (1997) describes how helpful SENCOs found such groups. She quotes a SENCO as saying: 'I like the feedback. I like being able to talk with people who understand.'

Quite apart from providing mutual support in understanding pupils' needs and how to meet these, SENCOs have also taken initiative to coordinate their Code of Practice procedures. This enabled them to be more effective in putting these into practice, and to manage the procedures with less difficulty. For example, some SENCOs decided on common approaches to formulating IEP documentation, so that there could be greater continuity in supporting pupils who moved between schools within or across phases.

JOINT APPOINTMENTS OF STAFF

Some groupings of schools make joint appointments of staff to support pupils with special educational needs. In our studies, we found a variety of appointments being made, such as learning support assistants (LSAs), a teacher to support pupils' transition from primary to secondary schools within a pyramid, a support teacher for pupils with specific learning difficulties, and a teacher to support pupils at the pre-school stage within a pyramid. These kinds of appointments were usually found in groupings of schools which had a more formal structure, through which the funding and line-management of such staff was organized.

One of the most significant joint appointments was that of a SENCO to all the schools in a grouping. The decision to make such an appointment seemed to be directly related to the aim of filling the 'gap' in provision mentioned at the start of this chapter. The purpose of the appointment was to have a member of staff 'owned' by the group, who could offer a higher level of expertise for meeting pupils' special educational needs than could be expected of other staff within the schools. This expertise had to include not only knowledge about pupils' special educational needs, but also ways to support individual teachers, LSAs and others working with the pupils. The SENCOs also often acted in a consultative role to heads in their planning of support systems within the schools. A further aspect of the role was the liaison with support services outside the school, and with the special needs administrators responsible for the statement procedure in the LEA.

The context of such joint SENCO appointments differed. In the rural 'Valley' pyramid grouping of schools, the primary schools were very small and had few staff. Consequently, it was impossible for the individual schools to have a member of staff who was sufficiently specialized to provide support for pupils. The pyramid decided to appoint a full-time SENCO who could serve all the four primaries and the small secondary school. As a result, the schools were able to employ a highly qualified SENCO which none of them could have afforded on its own. In addition, the joint SENCO is able to take responsibility for all the Code of Practice documentation, record-keeping and procedures which would otherwise fall as an additional administrative burden on the teaching headteachers. The joint SENCO is able to follow-up the children from primary to secondary school, and similarly to keep in touch with the children and their parents.

In other groupings of larger schools, which had themselves appointed teachers who included a SENCO role in their responsibilities, a shared appointment makes a more specialist source of expertise available. In these instances, the group SENCO acts as a support for the other SENCOs in the schools, and as a support for the development of special needs practice and policy. An important part of this latter role is to suggest ways in which schools can optimize the range of support, such as collaborative teaching, peer tutoring, parent support and the use of computer-assisted learning. The following are some of the ways in which these group SENCOs provided their support.

The group SENCOs usually had a programme of regular visits to the collaborating schools. The time they spent at each school would usually be agreed between the headteachers in each term or school year, and sometimes this arrangement would also determine the share of the cost of the appointment carried by each school (as described in Chapter 5). The school SENCOs found the support of the group SENCO very reassuring, and it certainly met some of the problems of isolation mentioned above. They were able to discuss their uncertainties in understanding and meeting individual pupils' special educational needs. The group SENCO might also be asked to look into the needs of particular pupils, especially if there was a question whether the pupil should be considered for a statement. Through the experience of working across all the member schools, the group SENCO was able to provide a kind of moderating role for the referral of pupils. The group SENCOs were often also asked to meet with the parents of pupils, in order to advise them and give them the benefit of their additional expertise. In one grouping of schools, the group SENCO enabled parents of children with specific learning difficulties to come together for advice about approaches to helping their children at home.

In groupings of schools which had set up resource centres, the group SENCOs usually take responsibility for these. Through the support they give in each school, they are able to find out what additional materials and equipment the school SENCOs need. Frequently, the ideas come from the group SENCOs themselves. This work sometimes leads to the group SENCOs setting up regular meetings between school SENCOs at the resource centres, where they can then share their questions and solutions, and where they can also be introduced to new approaches by the group SENCO. The group SENCOs thus support the school SENCOs with further professional development, both with regard to their direct work with children, and to keep them informed about special needs provision generally.

Because the group SENCOs are appointed to carry out their duties on a full-time basis, they are able to develop their own expertise and to keep themselves up to date, so that they can be an effective source of advice and support to the school SENCOs, and to the collaborating schools generally. For example, some of these group SENCOs are taking part in an electronic communications network. This network links them with other SENCOs throughout the country, and with specialists in the area of special educational needs (Wedell *et al.* 1997). The group SENCOs are thus able to gain advice and information from a wide range of sources, and pass this onto their colleagues in the collaborating schools.

In a number of groupings of schools which employ group SENCOs, these also take responsibility for the jointly appointed LSAs. On the basis of their knowledge of the pupils with special educational needs in each of the schools, they allocate the LSAs' time. The group SENCOs take responsibility for briefing the LSAs on the needs of the children, and advising them on ways of helping the children in consultation with the schools' own SENCOs. Either the schools' SENCOs or the group SENCOs will then work with the classroom teachers in whose lessons the LSAs provide support, to ensure that there is appropriate liaison between both. Having a SENCO who can take on this kind of responsibility ensures that the LSAs' time in the classroom is effectively used. As is well known, this liaison frequently fails to take place, with the result that the LSAs' potential support for the pupil is frustrated, and the LSAs' time is virtually wasted, along with the cost of employing them.

The above account of the benefits which can follow from schools appointing a group SENCO also indicates the potential dangers of such an arrangement. It would be very easy for schools and their teachers to absolve themselves from taking ownership of the special educational needs of their pupils, and to load all the responsibility onto the group SENCO. This point reflects back onto the nature of the schools' special educational needs policies. It also places a delicate responsibility on the group SENCOs to ensure that they are perceived primarily as facilitators of the schools' own response to the needs of their pupils. In other words, the group SENCOs have to be teachers who are skilled in providing indirect as well as direct support for pupils.

THE OUTCOMES FOR SCHOOLS, TEACHERS, PUPILS, AND PARENTS

Collaboration gave schools, particularly primary schools, an opportunity to develop their special needs policies to a level which is likely to be above the general run of schools. However, this is probably also due to the leadership of the headteachers of the participating schools, who initiated the collaboration in the first place. For many of the groupings of schools, collaborating to meet their pupils' special educational needs was just one aspect of their joint activities. The explicit focus on special needs inevitably made their special needs policies a live and active issue for all staff. In some schools, the approach to special needs was perhaps already more of an expression of an inclusive approach to the diversity of their pupils. Whether or not this was the case, it was likely that, as stated at the start of this chapter, the emphasis on collaboration rather than competition made it possible for the schools to develop a general attitude among teachers which enabled them to feel justified in attending to pupils' special educational needs. As a result, the effectiveness of teaching and learning was likely to be generally enhanced, and a wider range of pupils' needs met.

Because the schools were members of a collaborating group, their reputation for meeting their pupils' special educational needs was not something which they felt obliged to hide. So often schools which are effective in responding flexibly to pupils' needs find themselves in this ludicrous position, for fear that their reputation might affect their competitive status in relation to other local schools. Hopefully the move towards more relevant 'value-added' measures will enable these collaborating schools to be accorded the recognition they deserve for the higher levels of effective teaching and learning they achieve.

For teachers, the ethos of the collaborating schools tended to imbue their relationships with colleagues. Rather than keeping learning and teaching problems to themselves, they found that the climate in the schools encouraged them to share their problems and solutions. By establishing an ownership of pupils' special educational needs, the schools had also created an atmosphere in which teachers could feel supported. As one teacher was quoted in our previous study: 'I feel I shouldn't act alone in these things' (Lunt *et al.* 1994). The better communication between teachers helped them to realize that they were not alone in the teaching and management challenges posed by their pupils.

The further professional development opportunities which were provided in so many collaborative groupings of schools, both from their own SENCOs and from outside specialists, had a significant impact on the quality of teaching. It is well known that learning how to meet pupils' special educational needs in fact provides teachers with a greater competence in meeting the diversity of children's needs generally. In so far as our studies found that schools were providing further training to help teachers meet pupils' emotional and behaviour problems, there was also a feedback on approaches to class-group management in general. One of the teachers who had taken part in the observation in other schools mentioned above, reported: 'I feel an immeasurably better teacher through seeing other schools.'

Because of the emphasis on having SENCOs with the necessary expertise, teachers were also able to feel that they were adequately supported. Where SENCOs had the ability and commitment to seeing their role as influencing the way schools as a whole met their pupils' special educational needs, this often led to a graduated arrangement of support to match individual pupils' needs. Such an arrangement extended from SENCOs offering consultation and advice to teachers, to allocating LSA time to help teachers and pupils in class.

The collaboration between SENCOs and teachers enabled teachers to feel supported in adopting the 'problem-solving' approach to the teaching challenges which we mentioned above. Dyson and Millward (1997) have pointed out how crucial it is for teachers to feel that they have the scope to embark on this. SENCOs' support was based on their direct knowledge of pupils and of the particular strengths of the teachers concerned. In pyramid groupings of schools, the SENCOs' knowledge of the pupils and their background at the primary stage was often of crucial help in their advice to teachers in the secondary schools. The SENCOs' familiarity with pupils at the various stages of the Code in all the collaborating schools also enabled them to help teachers to see their pupils' needs in a wider perspective. On the one hand, this helped teachers to moderate the concern about a pupil's problems, and on the other hand, it enabled teachers to accept that a pupil's need required additional professional attention.

Where the groupings of schools had set up resource centres, teachers were likely to have a wider range of materials and equipment available to extend their teaching approaches. In the current financial constraints, this can be of considerable reassurance to teachers. It offers a crucial aid to flexible teaching, and saves teachers much time and effort in devising ways of meeting individual pupil needs. The in-service training which SENCOs can offer teachers in using the materials and equipment helps also to widen their repertoire of teaching methods.

Collaborative approaches among schools enable pupils to feel that their needs are being acknowledged. As teachers' competence increases, pupils can also feel more confident that their needs are being met. This is a direct consequence of the 'ownership' which teachers develop towards pupils' special educational needs. We were able to interview a number of pupils, and one of the impressions we gained was that they accepted the additional help and support as a normal part of their school's concern for them. This is in strong contrast to the stigma which is so often felt by pupils who receive help. Where groupings of schools make joint appointments of SENCOs, pupils were also much more likely to regard the additional help which the SENCOs gave to them individually or to their teachers as a normal part of the teaching/learning process.

It was notable that some groupings of schools had reduced the number of pupils whom they referred for statements. Admittedly, this was the express objective of some of the reallocation of resources to groupings of schools which has already been described in Chapter 5. However, the fact that it was achieved indicated that schools appeared to be more successful in meeting the individual needs of more pupils.

These outcomes inevitably made an impact on the parents of pupils with special educational needs. The sharing of responsibility for pupils' special educational needs among all the collaborating schools enabled the parents to feel that their children were receiving the same level of help in their particular schools as they would be offered in any of the other schools as well. Because special needs policies in the schools represented 'live' concerns, parents could also feel that the schools were committed to monitoring the effectiveness of the support which they were offering, and to continue to improve it as necessary. One of the most common causes of dissatisfaction among parents of pupils who have special educational needs is the feeling that the schools are not making sufficient effort on behalf of their children. Correspondingly, as will be mentioned in the next chapter, collaborative groupings of schools are in a much stronger position to influence the level of support which they obtain from the LEA and from any of the available support services.

Consequently, parents can feel that if, for example, a school considers that a pupil needs the additional support of a statement, such a decision is more likely to be heeded by the LEA.

It might be argued that some of the ways in which we found that schools increased the effectiveness of teaching and learning could have been achieved without collaboration. We would not dispute this. It is well known that, given the right leadership, a commitment to each individual pupil, and teamwork among staff, schools can go a long way towards building up the flexibility which meeting the diversity of their pupils' needs requires. However, such schools are the 'high achievers' which manage despite of, rather than because of, the system in which they operate. They are able to make progress towards resolving the problem of meeting individual pupils' needs within class groups.

The description we have given of the outcomes of collaboration shows how the normal run of schools can help each other to improve. Perhaps it is unfair to call them the 'normal run of schools', since they already have the determination to commit themselves to meeting the learning needs of all their pupils. They were able to recognize how much they could gain from collaboration, and were willing to risk foregoing some of their autonomy.

Although schools in the collaborative groupings which we studied undoubtedly were able to respond to a greater range of pupils and so make their contribution to filling the 'gap' mentioned at the start of the chapter, there were still pupils whose needs they could not meet on their own. In the next chapter, we will deal with the ways in which the outside support systems linked with collaborating schools, in order to maximize the help which they were able to offer.

7
SHARING EXPERTISE

In the previous chapter we considered the ways in which collaborating schools could increase their effectiveness in meeting pupils' special educational needs, so that they could contribute to closing the 'gap' in provision. In this chapter, we go on to look at how services outside the school can increase their responsiveness to pupils' special educational needs when schools come together in collaborative groupings. Although in the following we will be dealing primarily with how the function of services can be enhanced, we should never forget that, in the final analysis, our concern is for the children and young people and their families. This point was made well by a parent in a seminar on services:

> at individual family level, interagency working is frequently described as 'virtually non-existent'. Parents find themselves to be the keyworker who knows everyone involved with a child, and either communicates between them or prompts liaison. Ownership of responsibility is debated and then evaded.
>
> (Mallett 1996: 15)

Underlying the 'stages' of the Code of Practice is the principle of sharing expertise between all those involved in responding to pupils' special educational needs. Stages one and two are particularly focused on how expertise within the school and the pupil's home can be mobilized, as we discussed in the previous chapter. Many instances mentioned there involved the sharing of expertise among teachers and between SENCOs, teachers and learning support assistants (LSAs). One should also mention the sharing of expertise between parents and school staff. Wolfendale

(1992) has stressed the 'equivalent' expertise which parents have regarding their own children – expertise which clearly is of considerable importance to school staff in meeting pupils' special educational needs.

Stage 3 of the Code is the point at which the expertise of services outside the school is called in to play a direct part in supporting the school and the family in meeting individual pupils' needs. These services include both those within the educational sphere, such as specialist support teachers, educational psychologists and education welfare officers, and those from the other statutory services (Health and Social Services) and voluntary services. However, the Code of Practice (DfE 1994a) also makes clear that these services already have a contribution to make at the earlier stages: 'Outside specialists can play an important part in the very early identification of special educational needs and in advising schools on effective provision which can prevent the development of more significant needs' (para. 2.60). The emphasis on involving the services at stage 3 and subsequent stages sometimes seems to obscure this aspect of the Code's guidance.

Stages 4 and 5 (making a case for a statement to be maintained by the LEA, and the LEA's decision about agreeing to this) deal with statutory procedures. Although they are central to whether or not schools obtain additional resources, they are not stages where the outside services directly involve themselves with meeting pupils' special educational needs (as distinct from assessing them). However, the outcome of the statement decision clearly then has crucial significance for the part which the services play. It is well known that the contributions of the services are very much determined by the constrained funding available to them (Goacher *et al.* 1988).

We start by considering how services approach their task of helping to meet pupils' special educational needs. Just as the move towards collaboration among schools grew out of a reconsideration of ways to achieve effectiveness, this has also been a concern in relation to services. We start by considering general points about sharing expertise which apply both to the specialist education services (whether or not provided by the Education Authority) and to the other statutory and voluntary services. As Wedell (1995) has pointed out, sharing expertise has to apply not only to the nature, but also to the levels of expertise.

SHARING EXPERTISE AT VARIOUS LEVELS

Sharing expertise at various levels has been illustrated by the way in which services have recognized that they have to work indirectly as well as directly in meeting children and young people's needs. In other words, specialists have found it to be cost-effective to 'give away' their expertise to those who have the day-to-day responsibility for children and young people, by advising on teaching and other approaches. The description of the stages of the Code of Practice has, as mentioned above, too often given the impression that services are not involved in supporting schools until stage 3. Services which provide a consultative approach at earlier stages of schools' concern about pupils are able to help teachers, for example, to attend to particular needs through the way they interact with pupils in the classroom. As a result, the teachers can go some way both to meeting identified needs among pupils and also to preventing the development of needs in pupils. In this way, both schools and the services can help to fill the 'gap' in provision mentioned in the previous chapter.

Some services and the professional specialists working within them have often found it difficult to consider working in this indirect way. Paradoxically, this difficulty has sometimes arisen from the contraction of services resulting from the financial constraints in recent years. In the prevailing climate of accountability, the fact that it is difficult to 'count' indirect consultative work has made it harder for members of services to allocate time for this. For others, there has remained the misplaced fear that 'giving away' one's expertise might jeopardize one's job, or that it would take away the mystique from one's speciality.

Indirect work also requires specialists to travel to the places where children and young people's problems are found, and some have been fearful of emerging from their own territories, such as clinics. They have sometimes sought to justify this on the grounds of cost-effective use of their time, forgetting how frequently appointments at clinics are not kept. These specialists also fail to appreciate the wider preventative influence they can have by enhancing the supportive features of a child's or young person's context of daily life.

All of these points are relevant to collaboration between schools, because of the implication that it could be more cost effective for services to relate to groupings of schools. This was already pointed out in the discussion of clustering of schools in the Fish Report (ILEA 1985) on developing special needs service in the erstwhile Inner London Education Authority. The report pointed out that it would be more efficient for services to relate to groupings of schools in their localities, ranging from the pre-school to the post-school phases.

Focusing on localities enables staff of services to become familiar with the other resources which are available to children and young people with special educational needs and their families. These resources include both the actual and potential support in the environment, and even, more importantly, the personal characteristics of those with day-to-day responsibilities, such as the staff of schools. Members of services can come to know teachers, SENCOs and others, who can also discover in what ways the service members can be of help to them. Where the groupings of schools range across phases, service staff have the additional advantage of becoming familiar with the children in the course of their development. This familiarity enables service staff to see themselves as concerned with the children and young people in general in a locality, rather than just with referred 'cases' or 'problems' to which they are called.

In a great number of ways, when services develop their indirect work, they can increasingly make a preventative contribution, rather than spending all their efforts on crisis management. However, as has been pointed out in an Ofsted report (Ofsted 1997), the current financial constraints have severely depleted the staffing of services. To a great extent, the staff in many services have difficulty in 'getting their heads above water' sufficiently to be able to invest time in preventative work.

SHARING DIFFERENT KINDS OF EXPERTISE

So far, we have considered the sharing of levels of expertise. There has been a growing awareness of the need to share different forms of expertise. This point was highlighted in a recent study by the Centre for Research and Innovation of the OECD (OECD 1997). It was found that, in many countries, there was an increased awareness that the diverse needs of individual children and young people have to be seen as a whole. Focusing on one type of need within an individual, without considering other needs and strengths, was not likely to be effective, since the child's strengths and needs interacted with each other. Similarly, considering the child in isolation from the family was not likely to be effective. In other words, a holistic view of the child or young person was required. Such a view implies that there has to be a degree of coordination and collaboration between services, and some would even argue for the integration of services.

Coordination of services has, of course, to be adopted at all the layers of their organization. Over recent years, there has been much concern to promote collaboration and coordination between the main statutory services of Health, Education and Social Services. The recent legislation and consultation about the establishment of Children's Services Plans (CSPs), LEAs' Behaviour Support Plans, and Early Years Partnership Development Plans promote coordination within Local Authorities as an outcome of the 1989 Children Act and other subsequent legislation. Although in some areas coordination has already been achieved in many respects, notably between services for young children and infants, in other areas there are still many concerns to be overcome. In some local authorities, the participation of the education services in Children's Services Plans is still very marginal.

The awareness of the need for coordination between services to meet children's and young people's special educational needs is currently very apparent, and also forms an important feature of the Government's policy proposals in its Green Paper (DfEE 1997b). Hopefully, this accumulation of concern may actually bring about the necessary changes within the climate of administration from the ministerial departments down to the local service levels. However, one should not underestimate all the 'turf' and other worries which affect service managers at various levels when the issue of coordination is raised. Often, cooperation occurs between service workers in the local community long before the higher echelons are able to be persuaded of the potential efficiency benefits.

The OECD study mentioned above, emphasizes that service coordination has to occur in the local community if it is to make any impact for those who are intended to benefit. There has been discussion about how a 'local community' should be defined, but there is clearly a potential link here with the idea of the community which is served by a collaborative grouping of schools.

SHARING EXPERTISE WITHIN EDUCATION SERVICES

Sharing expertise within education services involves both specialist services and outreach support from special schools. First, we consider specialist education services.

SPECIALIST EDUCATION SERVICES

In our studies of groupings of schools, the services involved included the learning support services, the educational psychologists and the education welfare officers.

An important part of the background to the relationships between schools and the services was the changed funding arrangements following the education legislation introduced in the last years of the previous Government. As mentioned in earlier chapters, the introduction of the market economy ethos and the emphasis on delegating funding to individual schools greatly changed the relationships between LEA services and schools. The *SENCO Guide* (DfEE 1997c), which was based on studies of practice in schools, states:

> SENCOs saw ... their relationship with external agencies ... one of client-provider. They were becoming more assertive in specifying (on behalf of pupils) the services they needed from external agencies and the circumstances under which those services should be delivered.
>
> (para. 1.12)

As we have already pointed out in previous chapters, LEAs differed in the way they organized their support of schools, but there is no doubt that the general relationships had changed. This change has been acknowledged by the new government (DfEE 1997a): 'The role of LEAs has changed dramatically over the past decade ... LEAs must earn their place in the new partnership, by showing that they can add real value' (para. 17).

The same point is illustrated in the *SENCO Guide*: 'SENCOs were ... organising programmes of annual reviews at times which suited pupils, parents and themselves, rather than expecting timetabling to be determined solely by the convenience of external agencies' (para. 1.12).

Our studies of schools over recent years showed that this changed relationship was also found between groupings of schools and the LEA services. Interestingly, however, the change in relationship was a mutual one since, as mentioned in previous chapters, LEAs found that it was beneficial and more convenient for them to relate to groupings of schools. Indeed, as has already been mentioned, the groupings were often encouraged, if not instigated, by the LEAs themselves.

Some LEAs have left many of their services to fund themselves directly through 'service level agreements' with schools. These services have then been dependent on schools' demand for their support. Circular 6/94 (DfE 1994b) recommended, however, that LEAs should at least continue to maintain their services for children with minority special educational needs:

> In particular, the Secretary of State believes that LEAs should consider very carefully the case for retaining centrally low incidence SEN support services, notably those for pupils with visual, hearing and speech and language impairments.
>
> (para. 78)

Many LEAs heeded this advice, since children such as those with hearing and visual impairment might be scattered about in different schools, and any one school would have difficulty in affording the help which was needed. LEAs were, in any case, required to maintain educational psychologists.

One LEA in our study, as already mentioned in Chapter 3, had a particularly developed cooperative arrangement with collaborative groupings of schools in its area. We studied one of these groupings, and their organization has also been separately reported (Cade and Caffyn 1994). The LEA had set up support groups of staff such as educational psychologists and special needs service managers for mainstream schools to coordinate special needs resources in different areas of the county. Schools which had set up their own collaborative grouping in one area established a group of their SENCOs to consider and negotiate the additional help which the schools in the grouping needed. The negotiation included both funding and support provided by the LEA through its area support group. The support included contributions from a variety of staff: a special needs support teacher; an educational psychologist; a school welfare officer; a school nurse; and a classroom assistant. This group thus already contained members from a variety of services. Once the arrangements had been agreed, the SENCOs from the schools continued their contact with the support staff, and maintained regular meetings to monitor the help offered and to make any necessary modifications of the arrangements.

In some other groupings of schools in different LEAs, the liaison with support services was mediated by the SENCO jointly appointed by the collaborating schools. In one LEA, the learning support team had drawn up a rather complex gate-keeping arrangement for access to its support, largely because of the reduction in staffing which it had suffered. The jointly appointed SENCO, through her familiarity with the LEA learning support team members and their procedures, was able to gauge to what levels and forms of special educational needs the support team was likely to be willing to respond. As a result, the schools were able to make optimal use of the support team's services. In another grouping of schools, the jointly appointed SENCO had a more informal interaction with the educational psychologist and the LEA support teams, and so was able to consult and arrange for help according to the availability of the LEA staff concerned.

The large Black Horse grouping of schools described in Chapter 3 had been allocated a substantial range of LEA support staff. There were three special needs advisory support teachers, and there was also a special needs resource centre located in one of the primary schools with a half-time resource assistant. The management structure of heads and teachers oversaw the deployment of all these LEA staff. The LEA's special needs inspector played a key role in supporting the planning and arranging of this provision. Unfortunately, over successive years of increasing financial constraints, the number of LEA-provided staff was gradually reduced, but the collaborating schools still managed to make their own funding arrangements for some staff. The LEA still provides a special needs advisory teacher who has maintained the resource centre as a valuable pool of equipment and materials, and she has been active in developing these.

In some of the LEAs, the cooperation between groupings of schools and the LEA support staff also involved arrangements for in-service training. These arrangements enabled the LEA support staff to share their expertise with the staff of schools, and the contact with the schools gave them an opportunity to learn more about the schools and the needs of the pupils within them.

The Woodside grouping of schools mentioned in Chapter 3 provides a particularly interesting instance of the function of in-service training. This grouping of schools in an inner city area had close links with the teacher responsible for the school in the local children's hospital. The teacher had an expertise in emotional and behaviour problems, and helped the schools to form a group of voluntary helpers to support pupils with these difficulties within the group of schools. The hospital teacher provided training for both volunteers and teachers in the schools to carry out this support.

SPECIAL SCHOOL SUPPORT FOR MAINSTREAM SCHOOLS

For many years, from the Warnock Report (DES 1978) onwards, recommendations have been made that special schools should provide outreach support for mainstream schools. The report on the funding of special schools (Touche Ross 1990) stressed that they should always function as part of the general spectrum of provision within an LEA. More recently, the Government's Green Paper (DfEE 1997b) set out policy recommendations along the same lines, and also proposed that some special schools serving pupils with lower incidence needs should be given a brief for regional provision.

Within this pattern of outreach support, some special schools have developed particular links with mainstream schools in their locality, usually as part of their LEA's policy for special needs provision. Some of these instances are included in the survey reported in Chapter 2. In so far as these links follow from LEA initiatives, and usually involve provision for pupils with statements of special needs, they represent a 'top-down' organizational model. For example, the Green Paper mentions Round Oak School and Support Service (DfEE 1997b). This school and service was already described as exemplifying an approach to integration in the OECD/CERI study of integration in the UK (NFER 1992). The school and service was set up following the closure of two schools for children with moderate learning difficulties. Provision was made for children with statements of special needs, both within the new special school, and in eight local mainstream schools. Specialist teachers were appointed to work in the mainstream schools, but still remained members of the service provided by the special school. Within the mainstream schools, these teachers were responsible for the group of pupils with moderate learning difficulties who had been placed there – or who were already on the rolls of those schools. In addition to the support which the teachers gave to the designated pupils, they were also able to offer specialist advice and support more generally within the mainstream schools in consultation with the SENCOs of the schools.

Another example concerns a special school for children with physical impairment (Hill 1997). Here again, the closure of a school was used as an opportunity to set up provision in a set of primary and secondary schools. The school had for many years worked collaboratively with a secondary and a primary school within the LEA, and the LEA had made special provision for pupils placed in those schools. The new arrangement involves extension of this provision within the designated mainstream schools. The role of 'headteacher' of the original special school now takes the form of a specialist who is responsible for the dispersed staff and designated provision in the mainstream schools, which includes both the specialist teachers and the specialist 'plant' located in the mainstream schools.

Although both these examples differ from the prime examples of collaboration between schools which we have been discussing, because they represent a predominently 'top-down' model of collaboration, they are a very significant development towards inclusive provision for pupils with special educational needs. Descriptions of these collaborative arrangements indicate the complexity of the staff and other relationships which they entail within the schools. However, in principle, they provide a very significant development in making specialist support available to pupils with more severe forms of needs in mainstream schools.

SHARING EXPERTISE WITH NON-EDUCATION SERVICES

As mentioned above, the Fish Committee in its recommendations for meeting pupils in the Inner London Education Authority (ILEA 1985) stated as one of its objectives in promoting collaboration between groupings of schools:

to provide a focus for service delivery so that members of all services advising and supporting schools and associated tertiary provision, including health and social services, can deploy staff to work with a small group of schools. Schools in their turn would be enabled to work with a known group of supporting professionals.

(para. 3.16.24)

The Committee recognized the importance of achieving an effective level of communication between schools and the staff of services. As far as the services are concerned, there is a need to balance the economies of scale in the overall delivery of their services against the efficiency which can be gained from enhanced communication. This balance is obviously relevant to establishing a focus on the particular localities and communities served by groupings of schools.

Sharing of expertise can only be effective if those involved have an opportunity to come to know each other sufficiently well to be able to complement their respective contributions. Although the particular contribution of a member of any given service is ostensibly defined in that person's service terms, in practice what anyone offers is also very much determined by their particular experiences and personality. Effective sharing then depends on individuals having the opportunity to get to know each other, and the kinds of scope offered by each individual's context of work. Such mutual knowledge can only be achieved over a period of time, and requires continuity in the way service staff are deployed. This point came out very clearly in research carried out on collaboration between teachers and speech and language therapists, and also physiotherapists (Wright and Graham 1997). In her interviews with speech and language therapists and teachers who were working together to help individual pupils, Wright reports that both groups of professionals noted the gain in knowledge and information which they derived from such collaboration. Furthermore, both groups found that working together helped them to share concerns and to offer each other support with a resultant reduction in stress.

Unfortunately, the turmoil in service organization caused by the recent spate of legislation affecting all services has had a most disrupting effect on the relationship between members of services. Dessent (1996) refers to the 'atomization' of services:

There is an increasing emphasis on the purchaser/provider split in the development of community care arrangements, on the philosophy of internal markets, [on] the promotion of self-governing trust status and [on] the encouragement of GP fundholders.

People have changed their posts, been redesignated or have disappeared completely from services. It is hardly surprising that the *SENCO Guide* (DfEE 1997c) reports that:

SENCOs found it useful to spend time finding out about external agencies and the services they can offer. It was particularly helpful to identify key individuals and get to know them personally.

(para. 1.12)

In the current situation, any SENCO who achieved this can certainly be counted as fortunate. In many instances, service directories are out of date before they appear. Indeed, one of the recommendations in the report on SENCOs' use of electronic communication (NCET 1997) is that this might provide the only way for SENCOs to be updated from day to day on the staff of services and on their responsibilities.

None of the above points detracts, however, from the point made in the Fish Report (ILEA 1985) that groupings of schools form an obvious unit to which the statutory services of Health and Social Services could allocate members of their staff. Dessent (1996), in his discussion of options for partnership between health, education and social services, also refers to collaborative groupings of schools as a relevant 'focal point' for collaboration between these services. Groupings of schools, particularly those involving schools across phases, often delineate meaningful communities, expecially in rural areas. By 'meaningful', we mean groupings which relate to the way in which people's movements in their everyday lives are determined, and through which they establish their own network of contacts.

The effectiveness of service delivery is clearly crucially dependent on the take-up of services. It has been suggested in the OECD/CERI (OECD 1997) study that schools themselves might offer a strategic base where services for children and young people could make themselves available, and others have also made this point (McDonnell 1997). At the primary stages of children's development, parents are likely to come to schools to bring their children, therefore locating non-educational service staff in one or more collaborating primary schools would be likely to suit them.

Secondary schools differ in the extent to which they have a local intake of pupils. In some, it may well be that most pupils come from the local community, and this is particularly likely to apply in rural areas. Where pupils come from a wider area, there will still be a proportion whose families live in the area, and who are therefore likely to be served by other statutory services as well. However, older pupils would tend to prefer to refer themselves, so school-based 'one-stop' service provision might well make the uptake of the services more effective for them.

Locating services within schools would make it much easier for service staff to share their expertise with staff in schools. However, even where collaboration between services does not lead to their operating out of school bases, the emphasis on locating the services in communities is much more likely to facilitate links with collaborative groupings of schools. Some of the examples of collaboration between schools mentioned above included some instances of participation by non-education services. It would seem important that these kinds of considerations should be incorporated into the formation of Children's Services Plans and LEAs' Early Years Partnership Development Plans. Inter-service collaboration is relevant across the phases of children and young people's education, and should be extended into Youth Service Plans (Wylie, personal communication 1997) and LEAs' Behaviour Support Policies.

The OECD/CERI study (OECD 1997) listed the kinds of benefits which collaboration between services (including schools) yielded. The following are some of the points which emerged from the findings collected in projects in different countries:

> Professionals regard work in integrated settings as more satisfying, interesting, enjoyable and motivating, and less stressful. They believe that an integrated approach allows them to reach more clients and to achieve better results.
>
> Professionals who staff community-based integrated programmes say that they benefit from community participation and support, good relationships with community members and an increased ability to understand and adapt programmes to community needs.

> Middle managers... believe that integrated working practices achieve better outcomes for clients, reduce costs and provide more scope for prevention.
>
> Clients... are more likely to get all of the services they need, and to get them before a crisis point is reached. They are more likely to have a single and continuous contact point, and to receive consistent advice.
>
> Parents can benefit from integrated projects by taking advantage of their resources (e.g. school facilities) [and] improving their knowledge and self-esteem.
>
> (pp. 92–3)

There is clearly no dearth of appreciation that inter-agency collaboration and coordination is the only relevant way to achieve better provision for those with needs. Indeed, there are many more agencies between which collaboration should be extended – such as housing and law enforcement – if one were concerned also with the broader issues of social deprivation. However, our focus on sharing expertise to meet the special educational needs of children and young people and their families has already amply made the point.

The discussion in this chapter has offered some indications about how the sharing of expertise through inter-agency coordination and collaboration can be encouraged. It seems evident that encouragement and initiative has to come both 'top-down' from above and 'bottom-up' from below, in the same way that we found for collaboration between schools. As we have already mentioned, many of the recent and current government policy proposals call for collaboration and coordination at national, regional and local level. There is now an increasing demand for LEAs to produce development plans which include coordination. However, our studies have shown that the appreciation of autonomy among schools can also lead them to joint initiatives to influence service delivery. Hopefully, collaborative groupings of schools will increasingly lead them to make demands that support services – both educational and other – will work together to improve their contribution to meeting pupils' special educational needs. We will be looking more closely at these points in the final chapter.

8

THE WAY FORWARD

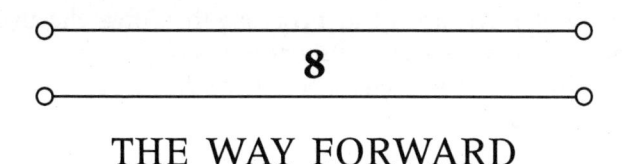

INTRODUCTION

The future policy context includes demands for greater effectiveness and higher standards. The press release on the launch of the White Paper in September 1997 'hailed the Education Summit hosted by the Prime Minister . . . as another clear indication that raising standards in schools is at the heart of Government policy' (DfEE 1997e). This policy drive is part of an international concern referred to in the introduction for an effectively educated population to support productivity levels and to achieve economic prosperity and competitiveness. In the UK, although there is a new Government, it is clear that there will be no significant shifts from the previous Government's education policy in its focus on standards and effectiveness, an emphasis on choice and diversity, and a market-driven orientation to the organization of education. However, there has been a significant shift, at least in aspiration, in terms of a commitment to greater inclusion of pupils with SEN. The new Government is clear in its commitment to greater inclusion. However, it could be said that these two goals (choice and diversity and greater inclusion) are built in part on potentially conflicting values: the more social values of inclusion versus the more individualistic values of choice and diversity. Inclusive values might imply cooperation and collaboration while the market-orientated values of choice might imply a more individualistic or competitive orientation. However, these values may come together in the search for greater effectiveness, and the aim to improve educational outcomes for all. Thus, for schools and LEAs to meet the needs of a wider group of pupils, they need to find ways of maximizing the effective use of their resources and increasing their own effectiveness in dealing with all pupils. Collaboration between schools is one way in which these goals may be achieved.

EDUCATIONAL INCLUSION

As has been mentioned, both in the UK and in the wider international context, there are moves for more inclusive policies in education, and the inclusion of more pupils with SEN in mainstream schools. These moves are apparent across the European Union and in North America where concerns about human rights, equal opportunities and the rights of disabled young people sit alongside concerns about the negative effects of educational exclusion.

This international commitment to inclusion was made explicit in 1994 by UNESCO in the Salamanca World Statement on Special Needs Education (UNESCO 1994), which stated that:

- education systems should be designed and educational programmes implemented to take into account the wide diversity of these characteristics and needs;
- those with special educational needs must have access to regular schools which should accommodate them within a child-centred pedagogy capable of meeting these needs;
- regular schools with this inclusive orientation are the most effective means of combating discriminatory attitudes, creating welcoming communities, building an inclusive society and achieving an education for all

(UNESCO 1994: viii)

Within the UK, recent policy documents and in particular the Green Paper (DfEE 1997b) support the Salamanca Statement:

We support the United Nations Educational, Scientific and Cultural organisation (UNESCO) Salamanca World Statement ... [which] calls on Governments to adopt the principle of inclusive education, enrolling children in regular schools, unless there are compelling reasons for doing otherwise

(p. 44)

The Green Paper expresses a goal to see more pupils with SEN in mainstream primary and secondary schools, and to 'promote the inclusion of children with SEN within mainstream schooling wherever possible', thus implying the need for a progressive extension of the capacity of mainstream schools to provide for children with a wider range of needs (p. 44). The measures proposed are intended to enhance mainstream schools' ability to include pupils with SEN.

However, the goal of inclusion poses a number of challenges to an already hard-pressed education system, and, although there has been a gradual trend in the UK towards including more disabled pupils in mainstream schools (Norwich 1997), this occurs alongside a significant increase in the exclusion of other pupils (Gillborn 1996; Parsons 1996; Parsons and Howlett 1996). Parsons and Howlett (1996) emphasize the need for schools to have the support of a wider society which cares for the well-being of all its members, a concern which sits uneasily alongside other more competitive aspects of the education context.

Recent education reforms in the UK have introduced a quasi-market situation for education (see Chapter 1), encouraging so-called parental choice and competition between schools for pupils and for positions in the league tables. Positions in the league tables have in the past been based on performance indicators such as test and examination scores, although now with some 'value-added' factors to be taken into account. However, the league tables and measures of effectiveness do not include indicators such as 'inclusiveness' or 'inclusivity', or measures which relate to the efficient use of resources for SEN or effective provision for pupils with SEN. In fact, pupils with SEN are still seen by many schools as less attractive, since they may require more support and may produce less successful examination results. The way in which additional resources are allocated by LEAs to schools may still be rewarding schools for 'failing' their pupils, by having a large number on a register of SEN, whether this be on the Code of Practice Stages or with statements of SEN. Thus the 'perverse incentive' may continue to lead to schools being rewarded for failing pupils and losing resources if they succeed in removing pupils from a SEN Register. In this way, competition between schools for resources encourages them to identify more pupils individually and to put them forward as in need of additional resources. This individual approach to the allocation of additional resources, rather than one which recognizes both the relativity of children's needs, and the interaction of factors in the child with factors in the school, may undermine attempts to enhance schools' overall ability to meet all children's needs by diverting resources away from attempts to develop whole school approaches towards a more individual 'remedial' type.

The challenge for schools and for communities is to develop more inclusive cultures (Thomas 1997) and to find strategies which will enable them to meet the diversity of needs of the pupils in their locality. 'Inclusive education can only flourish in a system which generates an inclusive ideology' (Corbett and Norwich 1997). As Thomas points out (1997), this notion resonates with wider notions of 'inclusivity' (Hutton 1995) and the 'stakeholder society' (Plender 1997), which allow a 'recognition of mutual obligations and expectations between the community and institutions such as schools, in a way that these institutions are reminded of their responsibilities and public duties' (Thomas 1997: 104). They resonate also with notions such as 'connexity' (Mulgan 1997) and 'communitarianism' (Etzioni 1996) to which we will return later, and the development of community responsibilities for schools and other institutions.

One way in which greater inclusion might be achieved is through 'specialist schools and families of schools' as mentioned by the White Paper, *Excellence in Schools* (DfEE 1997a, sections 4.13–15). The White Paper proposes 'new learning networks for developing specialisms within families of schools . . . as a collaborative programme which brings schools together, rather than as a competition for resources'. These collaborative arrangements would mean that groups of schools would work together, developing and sharing expertise to be used across the group of schools, a feature of many of the groups of schools in our studies of collaboration in relation to SEN. Under this model, special schools would become specialist schools, operating as resource bases for a group of schools and a local community, with all children on roll at a mainstream school, even though they might spend periods of time taking part in specialist education at the specialist school. A number of the groups of schools identified in our research already have the structure to develop this approach, which opens out the special school as a resource to local schools and potentially to the local community.

The Green Paper also explicitly mentions collaboration and seeks to develop structures which facilitate cooperation: 'effective collaboration between LEAs, social services departments and heath authorities is essential' (Green Paper, DfEE 1997b: 7.5). This is one of the models of collaboration envisaged by the Fish Committee when it reviewed provision for SEN in Inner London, and proposed that 'clusters' of schools should collaborate and that external agencies and services serving groups of schools would work together to meet the needs of the local community (ILEA 1985). Again, in its chapter on increasing inclusion, the Green Paper proposes 'special schools becoming part of cluster arrangements with primary and secondary schools' and 'guidance to schools on co-operative working' which might cover shared facilities, or shared teaching and non-teaching expertise (DfEE 1997b: 50). The implication is that schools will be better able to develop inclusive cultures and practices through collaboration rather than competition, and that special schools working together with mainstream schools provide a model for the sharing of expertise.

EDUCATIONAL EFFECTIVENESS

It is now well known that research into school effectiveness over the last two decades has demonstrated that schools make a significant difference to children's progress and attainment (Mortimore *et al.* 1988; Barber 1996; Sammons *et al.* 1997), and that effective schools promote the highest outcomes for the maximum number of students, regardless of the background of these students (Mortimore 1995). It has been argued by Ainscow (1991), among others, that, by improving overall conditions, a school develops a wider range of responses to pupils who experience difficulties in their learning, and that schools which are effective are so with all pupils, including those with SEN. Ainscow (1997) argues for a 'pedagogy of inclusion', which includes an emphasis on teamwork and on teachers sharing ideas, working alongside each other, and observing each other's practices, and on fostering collaborative ways of working.

COLLABORATION AND EDUCATIONAL EFFECTIVENESS

There have been a number of studies which have shown that mainstream schools can increase their effectiveness in meeting pupils' SEN if they collaborate (Dyson and Gains 1993; Lunt *et al.* 1994). Some of the examples described earlier in the book have demonstrated the different ways in which schools have collaborated to share and enhance their expertise and their capacity to meet pupils' special educational needs.

The Green Paper (DfEE 1997b) states in chapter 1: 'By 2002 the policies set out in *Excellence in Schools* for raising standards, particularly in the early years, will be beginning to reduce the number of children who need long-term special educational provision.'

This statement indicates a demand for greater educational effectiveness for all pupils which in turn will benefit pupils with SEN. The demand for greater effectiveness is part of a current concern across the developed world about effectiveness generally in schools (NCE 1993; Barber 1996; Green 1997). This may be seen particularly in relation to the consequences of social problems (e.g. Dyson 1997; Mortimore and Whitty 1997), and the growing number of pupils experiencing difficulties in behaviour and emotional problems leading to increasing numbers of pupils being excluded from school (e.g. Parsons 1996). Inclusion needs to be seen not only as a process for including pupils with disabilities in mainstream schools, but also as a process of making mainstream schools more inclusive for *all* pupils, including those in danger of social exclusion. In the UK, the setting up of a Social Exclusion Unit acknowledges the reality and the urgency of these problems; in a speech at the launch of the Unit, Prime Minister Tony Blair argued that attempts to tackle social problems in isolation will fail, and that schools cannot on their own be expected to solve society's ills: 'they need the backing of parents and the community, and they need the help of all the different agencies that work with young people' (Gardiner 1997). Similarly, the European Union includes among its priorities the development of strategies which will reduce social exclusion among young people.

> More than ever, failure at school begets social failure, which means a life of uncertainty, marginalisation and dependence on the structures of social assistance. As the level of education is a factor of the utmost importance to economic, social and political integration, we must ensure that the mechanisms which give rise to exclusion among young people are eliminated ... It is therefore necessary to reassert the

individual's right to education. This right to education implies the right of everyone to receive the basic knowledge and training required to enable him to find employment and to play a full part in society.

(European Commission 1994: 9)

These concerns also include a recognition of the need for a wider view of effectiveness to cover broader curriculum aims which need to be reflected in the review of the National Curriculum, and its relevance to all children. The notion of an entitlement curriculum needs to be seen alongside a pedagogy for inclusion, as mentioned above, in such a way that all children have access to learning, and that all children are enabled to make progress, and do not become victims in the drive to improve standards in particular in examination results. Our focus on the effective meeting of pupils' SEN is part of a general concern for effective curriculum organization for all pupils (see Weston et al. 1992), as well as the demand for adequate expertise to meet the specific features of the range of SEN. For the majority of pupils with SEN, such expertise will be provided by teachers in mainstream schools, supported where appropriate and necessary by specialist support services based in the LEA, health or social services or in the community. However, a small minority of pupils may always need considerable support of specialist teachers and professionals from other services based locally or regionally; the Government's Green Paper (DfEE 1997b) makes a commitment to reducing the number of pupils in need of such permanent support.

Thus, the theme of collaboration is part of a general recognition that the complexity of pupils' needs demands the combined effort of a number of relevant services which include education, health and social services and other agencies such as the voluntary sector. The requirement for Children's Services Plans by Department of Health Regulations forms part of this recognition. Writing about services for children, Bilton and Jones (1994), quoted by Russell (1997: 39), emphasize the need for 'a value-led approach, which leads to a comprehensive vision of services for children... the current changes should be acknowledged to be both opportunities and challenges in terms of integration and principled planning'. Russell suggests further that in looking at the development of children's services plans, 'the department [of Health] recognised that cooperation was part of a hierarchy of collaborative working relationships which started with *communication* and progressed through *consultation* towards *collaboration . . . bi-lateral planning . . . joint planning . . . joint commissioning*' (Russell 1997: 39).

Specific recognition of the need and potential for collaboration is demonstrated in the setting up of Education Action Zones, following the Government White Paper (DfEE 1997a). A typical zone is likely to have two or three secondary schools, with their feeder primaries and associated SEN provision, and involving representatives from the local community. It is logical that non-education professionals and other agencies will work together within an Education Action Zone such that a coordinated approach to providing children's services becomes possible. Early Years Development Plans expected of all LEAs from April 1998 imply collaboration: in announcing 'a fresh start in early years education' Secretary of State David Blunkett stated: 'there will be no more destructive competition. It will be replaced by close consultation and co-operation between parents, providers, local education authorities and the private and voluntary sectors' (DfEE Press Release 115/97). Further initiatives, such as the requirement for Behaviour Support Plans and for LEA Literacy Strategies imply a cooperative and coordinated approach to the task of improving the effectiveness of schools for all children. Moss and Petrie (1997: 12) go further and propose 'a concept of a civic society based on a number of interconnected social values, including social cohesion and inclusion, reciprocity and democratic participation. Such values are not necessarily incompatible with more individualistic values, including choice. The important issue is achieving a proper balance between civic and individualistic values.' The notion of values is key here (Lindsay 1997), and connects with the collaborative and social values found in a number of the collaborative schools that we studied. Such proposals contain the potential for community building and social inclusion, and for the development of inclusive communities which will support inclusive schools.

ECONOMY OF SCALE

In addition to the question of values and collaborative ethos, collaboration may be seen as meeting the demands of economy of scale in times of financial constraint. It is clear that schools are not able to meet all pupils' needs on their own, and that it may be considered financially inefficient for all schools to make provision for all pupils. If schools are to be enabled to include a wider range of pupils with different SEN, there will need to be some consideration given to economies of scale and shared resources. It is possible to predict with some accuracy the incidence of so-called 'minority' or 'low-incidence' special needs, such as disabilities of sight and severe physical disability, and to plan for their provision; it is also possible to estimate the numbers of pupils with learning difficulties in a given locality. Collaboration between schools provides a level of resource allocation which permits economies of scale, and which offers a level of organization between the level of the school and the level of the local authority, while still maintaining schools' autonomy (Gray and Dessent 1993).

In this way, it is possible to envisage levels of organization of provision which enable children's needs to be met in their locality, but which may be provided at school, group of schools, local authority or regional level according to the nature and frequency of the need. With local government reorganization and the formation of a number of small unitary authorities, it is likely that some provision will require planning at the regional level, an issue also recognized by the Green Paper (DfEE 1997b), and by developments in Children's Services Plans which acknowledge the need for planning at different levels (Russell 1997). There are a number of services which are likely to be provided at the regional level, and it is clear from the Green Paper that reorganization is envisaged probably to incorporate planning and decision-making at different levels, and involving collaborative arrangements, both between schools and services. However, although it is clear that collaboration between schools and among services may foster inclusive values and the development of a 'civic society' (Moss and Petrie 1997) and may permit economies of scale, it is also clear that there may be dilemmas implied by collaboration.

THE DILEMMAS

Norwich (1996: 101) points out the tensions found within education generally as revolving round the interplay between the values of equality, individuality, social inclusion and practicability; these must be added to the tensions implicit now in all education and social welfare systems between competition and collaboration, and the importance emphasized above of 'achieving a proper balance between civic and individualistic values' (Moss and Petrie 1997: 12), or between the values of inclusion and the values of choice and diversity already mentioned above. Looking at different models of local government, Ball *et al.* (1997) have identified three models: the first where community needs and local political goals are high priorities; the second where maintenance of service provision and support for schools are high priorities; and the third where cost reduction and performance and monitoring are high priorities. These different priorities and models illustrate some of the tensions in the provision of services, particularly in the context of the uncertainties resultant, in recent years from local government reorganization and legislative change. Different levels of collaboration also raise a dilemma, because of the coordinating implications of higher levels over lower levels, and because of the role of regional bodies, such as local authorities, in relation to autonomous institutions, such as schools. The model of purchaser-provider, introduced extensively into the Health Service, but also extended to the Education Service, has succeeded to an extent in reversing the power balance between schools and LEAs. This may make the coordinating, monitoring and planning role of an LEA more difficult when it is also the provider of services which schools may or may not wish to purchase. Under LMS, schools have attained a high degree of autonomy together with considerable responsibilities. Similarly, unitary authorities have also attained autonomy and independence from a larger regional authority and have sought to develop their own services and their own structures. Unitary authorities are thus faced with the challenge and opportunity to create 'a new and collective approach to children's services' (Russell 1997: 42). However, it is important not to underestimate some of the difficulties in multi-professional collaboration and inter-agency working as the professional 'territoriality' and the 'potential for inter-professional rivalry over roles and responsibilities' (Dessent 1996; Russell 1997).

In this sense, therefore, collaboration could be said to go against the idea of the autonomy of schools in relation to LEAs and the autonomy of unitary authorities in relation to regionalization, also undermining the principles of competition between individual schools and parental choice which are believed to be one of the cornerstones in the drive to improve schools and to raise standards. However, our studies and discussions have shown that schools are willing to collaborate and to operate beyond a competitive ethos, provided that the advantages are perceived to outweigh the disadvantages, and that the costs of collaboration (usually in time and loss of autonomy) are exceeded by the benefits (often of confidence, support, expertise and some resources).

There is clear evidence that some LEAs already collaborate in meeting SEN by sharing service delivery, particularly with 'minority' special needs. In some areas Children's Services Plans indicate that collaboration can occur between services, and that this can improve efficiency. Our discussion of the collaborative process during these studies with schools indicates some of the factors which influence their willingness to collaborate. These factors include: the facilitative role of the LEA; financial incentives provided by the LEA; economies of scale made possible by shared resources; staff support developed through a shared culture and professional development; and, in some cases, shared planning and decision making in relation to additional resources for SEN. It was clear that some of the more lasting and possibly more rewarding collaborative groups had managed to achieve a balance of 'bottom-up' and 'top-down' initiation and maintenance which meant that the schools' willingness to take ownership and responsibility through collaboration was balanced by the LEAs' support and facilitation, frequently in the context of financial incentives within funding policies. Again, these LEA policies were frequently aimed at increasing inclusion, and collaboration between schools was one way in which schools could enhance their own capacity to meet a wider range of pupils' needs.

THE NEW POLICY CLIMATE

The Labour Government has sought to define a new policy culture with an emphasis on collaboration and partnership. Concepts such as 'trust' (Fukuyama 1995); 'connexity' (Mulgan 1997); 'communitarianism' (Etzioni 1996); 'stakeholder society' (Hutton 1995; Plender 1997), and 'inclusivity' (Thomas 1997) are seen as providing ways forward to meet the needs of individuals and society in the future. Barber (1997) quotes Fukuyama in suggesting that 'there is no necessary trade-off... between community and efficiency; those who pay attention to community may indeed become the most efficient of all' (p. 12). In his book entitled *Connexity*, Mulgan suggests that 'a more connected culture does indeed become more attuned to difference... the most successful orders turn out to be those based on mutual transparency, trust-building and common responsibility' (p. 17). These ideas have found a resonance with the present Government to give a new direction to policy including that for education. In parallel, there are developments in forms of local and regional government, and new notions of responsibility and accountability (Ball *et al.* 1997); these are developed together with an awareness of the financial constraints and competing demands of the welfare state and public sector provision. As mentioned above, the policy goals and thus the challenges for the education system are on the one hand higher standards and excellence for all, while on the other hand more inclusion and more inclusive schools, while maintaining parental choice and diversity. In this climate, we have shown that there is a considerable number of groups of schools which choose to collaborate, and which experience the benefits of collaboration in their efforts to meet pupils' special educational needs.

IMPLICATIONS FOR SCHOOLS

Our studies and discussion have shown that a collaborative ethos also affects the way that individual schools themselves operate and that there is a collaborative ethos within, as well as between, schools, which supports teachers and promotes a more inclusive approach. This finding is also supported by studies of school effectiveness, which demonstrate the benefits of collaboration within schools, and studies of teacher support teams, which show the benefits of collaboration between teachers in one school (Norwich and Daniels 1997).

A more inclusive society and more inclusive schools demand major developments in how schools perceive and meet their responsibilities towards their pupils, and to the communities they serve. For schools to be more inclusive, requires a culture shift in attitudes and expectations and realization that inclusion means adaptation of the school to meet pupils' needs rather than for the pupils to fit into the school. This culture shift is in line with many of the value positions espoused in the new policy climate and put forward by Moss and Petrie (1997) in their concept of a civic society. Thus there is a recognition that each community is likely to have a number of vulnerable pupils and young people, for whom it has the main responsibility. It is possible for schools to collaborate both formally and informally to share expertise and resources, to take collective responsibility for the more vulnerable pupils, and to develop a more collaborative ethos to promote educational and social inclusion within mainstream schools. In this structure, special schools will continue to have a role as specialist schools (along the lines proposed in the Education Action Zones, and suggested in the Green Paper) serving as a resource and a support to mainstream schools with pupils with SEN, and mainly operating as outreach and resource bases. Within a group of schools, the specialist school would provide the base for a range of services both educational and non-educational, with additionally resourced mainstream schools providing the base for the pupils themselves. It is thus possible to envisage an effective means of meeting SEN through collaboration among schools which enhances the capacity of individual schools as well as the local community to make effective provision for all pupils.

CONCLUSION

Collaboration is a major means to achieve cost effectiveness in the provision to meet pupils' SEN in mainstream schools. At a financial level, this means that resources may be allocated to a group of schools, and used in part through the local specialist school(s) and in part to resource mainstream schools to meet the needs of individual pupils in the community. However, at another level, cost effectiveness is also achieved through collaboration by maximizing the skills and expertise of teachers, for example through developing networks of SENCOs and other staff, and through the development of a network of support and expertise across the schools which reduces the need for individual support of teachers and pupils. There is also the recognition that, if this is to lead to more cost-effective outcomes for pupils, including those with SEN, the values underlying cost effectiveness have to reflect a wider view of the aims of education and 'effectiveness' in schools than is currently associated with concepts of 'standards', in such a way that indicators of schools' effectiveness include also their effectiveness at meeting the needs of the diverse group of pupils in the locality. This means that schools and the community will take responsibility and ownership for all the pupils in the locality, drawing on a sense of collective responsibility and collaboration to enhance their own effectiveness and to promote a civic society and an inclusive education system.

REFERENCES

Adler, M. (1997) Looking Backwards to the future: parental choice and education policy. *British Educational Research Journal,* 23 (3): 297–313.
Ainscow, M. (1991) *Effective Schools For All.* London: David Fulton.
Ainscow, M. (1993) *Towards Effective Schools for All.* Stafford: National Association for Special Educational Needs.
Ainscow, M. (1997) Towards inclusive schooling. *British Journal of Special Education,* 24 (1): 3–6.
Audit Commission (1988) *Delegation of Management Authority to Schools.* London: HMSO.
Audit Commission (1994) *The Act Moves on: Progress in Special Educational Needs.* London: HMSO.
Audit Commission/HMI (1992a) *Getting in on the Act. Provision for Pupils with Special Educational Needs: The National Picture.* London: HMSO.
Audit Commission/HMI (1992b) *Getting the Act Together: Provision for Pupils with Special Educational Needs.* London: HMSO.
Ball, S. J. (1987) The Micro-Politics of the School, London: Routledge.
Ball, S. J., Vincent, C. and Radnor, H. (1997) Into confusion: LEAs, accountability and democracy. *Journal of Educational Policy,* 12 (3): 147–63.
Barber, M. (1996) *The Learning Game.* London: Victor Gollancz.
Barber, M. (1997) *How to do the Impossible: A Guide for Politicians with a Passion for Education.* Inaugural lecture. London: Institute of Education.
Barnard, N. (1997) Overhaul expected for special needs. *Times Educational Supplement,* 17 October.
Benford, M. (1988) Beyond clustering. *Education,* 23 September: 294–5.
Bowe, R. and Ball, S. J. with Gold, A. (1992) *Reforming Education and Changing Schools.* London: Routledge.
Bridges, D. and Husbands, C. (eds) (1996) *Consorting and Collaborating in the Education Market Place.* London: Falmer Press.
Cade, L. and Caffyn, R. (1994) The King Edward VI family: an example of clustering in Nottinghamshire. *Support for Learning,* 9 (2): 83–8.

Cade, L. and Caffyn, R. (1995) Family planning for special needs: the role of the Nottinghamshire Family Special Needs Co-ordinator. *Support for Learning* 10 (2): 70–4.

Coldron, J. and Boulton, P. (1991) 'Happiness' as a criterion of parental choice of school. *Journal of Education Policy*, 6 (2): 169–78.

Coopers & Lybrand (1996) *The SEN Initiative-Managing Budgets for Pupils with Special Educational Needs*. London: Coopers & Lybrand.

Corbett, J. and Norwich, B. (1997) Special Needs and Client Rights: the changing social and political context of special educational research. *British Educational Research Journal*, 23 (3): 379–89.

Creemers, B. P. M. (1994) *The Effective Classroom*. London: Cassell.

DES (1978) *Special Educational Needs: Report of the Committee of Enquiry into the Education of Handicapped Children and Young People*, Warnock Report. London: HMSO.

DES (1988) *Education Reform Act: Local Management of Schools*, Circular 7/88. London: DES.

Dessent, T. (1996) *Options for Partnership Between Health, Education and Social Services*. Stafford: National Association for Special Educational Needs.

DfE (1992) *Choice and Diversity*, White Paper. London: HMSO.

DfE (1993) *Education Act*. London: HMSO.

DfE (1994a) *Code of Practice on the Identification and Assessment of Special Educational Needs*. London: HMSO.

DfE (1994b) *The Organisation of Special Educational Provision*, Circular 6/94. London: DfE.

DfEE (1997a) *Excellence in Schools*, White Paper. London: The Stationery Office.

DfEE (1997b) *Excellence for All Children: Meeting Special Educational Needs*, Green Paper. London: The Stationery Office.

DfEE (1997c) *The SENCO Guide*. London: DFEE.

DfEE (1997d) *The Implementation of the National Literacy Strategy*. London: Department for Education and Employment.

DfEE (1997e) *Way Forward for Early Years Education Announced*. London: DfEE.

DfEE (1998) *Education Bill*. London: HMSO.

Dyson, A. (1997) Social and educational disadvantage: reconnecting special needs education. *British Journal of Special Education*, 24 (4): 152–7.

Dyson, A. and Gains, C. (1993) Special needs and effective learning: towards a collaborative model for the year 2000, in A. Dyson and C. Gains (eds) *Rethinking Special Needs in Mainstream Schools Towards the Year 2000*. London: David Fulton.

Dyson, A. and Millward, A. (1997) The reform of special education or the transformation of mainstream schools?, in S. J. Pijl, C. J. W. Meijer and S. Hegarty (eds) *Inclusive Education*. London: Routledge.

Dyson, A., Millward, A. and Lin, M. (1997) *The Implementation of the Code of Practice: The Role of the Special Educational Needs Coordinator*. Newcastle upon Tyne: University of Newcastle upon Tyne.

Etzioni, A. (1996) *The New Golden Rule: Community and Morality in a Democratic Society*. London: Profile Books.

European Commission (1994) *Measures to Combat Failure at School: A Challenge for the Construction of Europe*. Luxembourg: Office for Official Publications of the European Communities.

Evans, J. and Lunt, I. (1994) *Markets, Competition and Vulnerability: Some Effects of Recent Legislation on Children with Special Educational Needs*. London: Tufnell Press.

Evans, J. and Vincent, C. (1997) Parental choice and special education, in R. Glatter, P. Woods and C. Bagley (eds) *Choice and Diversity in Schooling: Perspectives and Prospects*. London: Routledge.

Fish, J. and Evans, J. (1995) *Managing Special Education: Codes, Charters and Competition*. Buckingham: Open University Press.

Fletcher-Campbell, F. (1996) *The Resourcing of Special Educational Needs*. Slough: NFER.

Fukuyama, F. (1995) *Trust: The Social Virtues and the Creation of Prosperity*. London: Hamish Hamilton.

Gains, C. (ed.) (1994) Collaborating to meet special educational needs. *Support for Learning*, 9 (2), special issue.

Gallacher, N. (1995) Partnerships in education, in A. Macbeth, D. McCreath and J. Aitchison (eds) *Collaborate or Compete? Educational Partnerships in a Market Economy*. London: Falmer Press.

Gardiner, J. (1997) Blair hugs the limelight. *Times Educational Supplement*, 19 December.

Gewirtz, S., Ball, S. J. and Bowe, R. (1995) *Markets, Choice and Equity in Education*. Buckingham: Open University Press.

Giddens, A. (1991) *Modernity and Self-Identity: Self and Society in the Late Modern Age*. Cambridge: Polity Press.

Gillborn, D. (1996) *Exclusions from School*. Institute of Education Viewpoint 15. London: Institute of Education.

Glatter, R., Woods, P. and Bagley, C. (eds) (1997) *Choice and Diversity in Schooling: Perspectives and Prospects*. London: Routledge.

Goacher, B., Evans, J., Welton, J. and Wedell, K. (1988) *Policy and Provision for Special Educational Needs*. London: Cassell.

Goddard, D. and Clinton, B. (1994) Learning networks, in S. Ranson and J. Tomlinson (eds) *School Co-operation: New Forms of Local Governance*. London: Longman.

Goldstein, H. *et al.* (1996) A multi-level analysis of school examination results. *Oxford Review of Education*, 19 (4): 425–33.

Gray, P. and Dessent, T. (1993) Getting our act together. *British Journal of Special Education*, 20 (1): 9–11.

Green, A. (1997) *Education, Globalization and the Nation State*. London: Macmillan.

Gross, J. (1996) The weight of parental evidence: Parental advocacy and resource allocation to children with statements of special educational needs. *Support for Learning*, 11 (1): 3–8.

Guardian (1996) Riding out the storm, *The Guardian*, 6 November.
Halpin, D., Power, S. and Fitz, J. (1997) Opting into the past? Grant-maintained schools and the reinvention of tradition, in R. Glatter, P. Woods and C. Bagley (eds) *Choice and Diversity in Schooling: Perspectives and Prospects*. London: Routledge.
Hill, G. (1997) 'The Vale Development Project', Paper delivered at the NICOD Educational Symposium, Belfast.
Hopkins, D. and Harris, A. (1997) Improving the quality of education for all. *Support for Learning*, 12 (4): 147–51.
Housden, P. (1993) *Bucking the Market: LEAs and Special Needs*. Stafford: National Association for Special Educational Needs.
Hutton, W. (1995) *The State We're In*. London: Vintage Press.
ILEA (1985) *Educational Opportunities for All?*, The Fish Report. London: Inner London Education Authority.
Jones, F. (1997) How can I promote and improve local support groups of special needs coordinators in a shire LEA? *Worcester Papers in Education*, 2: 14–20.
Lawton, S. (1992) Why Restructure? An international survey of the roots of reform. *Journal of Education Policy*, 7 (2): 139–54.
Lee, T. (1996) *The Search for Equity: Funding of Additional Needs Under LMS*. Aldershot: Avebury.
LeGrand, J. and Bartlett, W. (eds) (1993) *Quasi-Markets and Social Policy*. Basingstoke: Macmillan.
Levačić, R. (1995) *Local Management of Schools: Analysis and Practice*. Buckingham: Open University Press.
Lewis, A., Neill, S. and Campbell, R. J. (1996) *The Implementation of the Code of Practice*. Coventry: University of Warwick.
Lindsay, G. (1997) Values, rights and dilemmas. *British Journal of Special Education*, 24 (2): 55–9.
Lindsay, G. and Thompson, D. (eds) (1997) *Values into Practice in Special Education*. London: David Fulton.
Lunt, I. and Evans, J. (1994) *Allocating Resources for Special Educational Needs: Policy Options for Special Education in the 1990s*. Stafford: NASEN.
Lunt, I., Evans, J., Norwich, B. and Wedell, K. (1994) *Working Together: Inter-school Collaboration for Special Needs*. London: David Fulton.
Macbeth, A., McCreath, D. and Aitchison, J. (eds) (1995) *Collaborate or Compete? Educational Partnerships in a Market Economy*. London: Falmer Press.
Mallett, B. (1996) The changing role of parents, *Special Educational Policy Options Group, Provision for Special Educational Needs from the Perspectives of Service Users*. Stafford: National Association for Special Educational Needs.
Marsh, A. J. (1995) The effect of school budgets of different non-statemented indicators within a common funding formula. *British Educational Research Journal*, 21 (1): 99–115.

Marsh, A. J. (1997) *Current Practice for Resourcing Additional Educational Needs in LEAs*. Slough: Educational Management Information Exchange, NFER.

McDonnell, V. (1997) The needs of children and families, in S. Wolfendale (ed.) *Working with Parents of SEN Children after the Code of Practice*. London: David Fulton.

Meijer, C. and Stevens, L. (1997) Restructuring special education provision, in S. J. Pijl, C. J. W. Meijer and S. Hegarty (eds) *Inclusive Education*. London: Routledge.

Mortimore, P. (1995) *Effective Schools: Current Impact and Future Potential*. The Director's Inaugural lecture. London: Institute of Education.

Mortimore, P. and Whitty, G. (1997) *Can School Improvement Overcome the Effects of Disadvantage?* London: Institute of Education.

Mortimore, P., Sammons, P., Stoll, L., Lewis, D. and Ecob, R. (1988) *School Matters*. Wells: Open Books.

Moss, P. and Petrie, P. (1997) *Children's Services: Time for a New Approach*. London: Institute of Education.

Mulgan, G. (1997) *Connexity. How to Live in a Connected World*. London: Chatto & Windus.

National Commission on Education (NCE) (1993) *Learning to Succeed*. London: Heinemann.

National Curriculum Council (NCC) (1989) *A Curriculum for All: Special Educational Needs in the National Curriculum*. York: NCC.

National Foundation for Educational Research (NFER) (1992) *OECD/CERI Project: Integration in the School, Reports of Case Studies in the UK*. Slough: NFER.

NCET (1997) *SENCOs Sharing Solutions: An Evaluation of the SENCO Electronic Communications Project*. Coventry: National Council for Educational Technology.

Nichol, M. (1997) The role of the Statement in DfEE (1997) *The Code of Practice Two Years On: Report of the National Conferences Held in London and York*. London: DfEE.

Norwich, B. (1996) Special needs education or education for all: connective specialisation and ideological impurity. *British Journal of Special Education*, 23 (3): 100–4.

Norwich, B. (1997) *A Trend Towards Inclusion*. Bristol: CSIE.

Norwich, B. (1998) *Future Policy for Special Educational Needs: In Response to the Green Paper*. Stafford: National Association for Special Educational Needs.

Norwich, B. and Daniels, H. (1997) Teacher Support Teams for Special Educational Needs: evaluating a teacher-focused support scheme. *Educational Studies*, 23 (1): 5–23.

Observer (1997) Observer schools guide reveals the successes that league tables leave behind, *Observer*, 23 November.

OECD (1995) *Our Children at Risk*. Paris: OECD.

OECD (1997) *Successful Services for our Children and Families at Risk*. Paris: OECD.
Ofsted (1996a) *Exclusions from Secondary Schools, 1995–6*. London: HMSO.
Ofsted (1996b) *Promoting High Achievement for Pupils with Special Educational Needs in Mainstream Schools*. London: HMSO.
Ofsted (1997) *The SEN Code of Practice Two Years On*. London: Ofsted.
Parsons, C. (1996) Permanent exclusions from school in England in the 1990s: trends, causes and responses. *Children and Society*, 10: 177–86.
Parsons, C. and Howlett, K. (1996) Permanent exclusions from school: a case where society is failing its children. *Support for Learning*, 11 (3): 109–12.
Pijl, S. and Meijer, C. (1991) Does integration count for much? An analysis of the practices of integration in eight countries. *European Journal of Special Needs Education*, 6 (2): 100–11.
Plender, J. (1997) *A Stake in the Future: The Stakeholding Solution*. London: Nicholas Brealey Publishing.
Powell, W. W. (1991) Neither market nor hierarchy: network forms of organisation, in J. Thompson, J. Frances, R. Levačić and J. Mitchell (eds) *Markets, Hierarchies and Networks: The Coordination of Social Life*. London: Sage.
Pugach, M. C. (1995) On the failure of imagination in inclusive schooling. *Journal of Special Education*, 29 (2): 212–23.
Ranson, S. (1992) Towards the learning society. *Educational Management and Administration*, 20 (1): 68–79.
Ranson, S. (1994) *Towards the Learning Society*. London: Cassell.
Ranson, S. and Tomlinson, J. (eds) (1994) *School Co-operation: New Forms of Local Governance*. London: Longman.
Riddell, S. and Brown, S. (1994) *Special Educational Needs Policy in the 1990s: Warnock in the Market Place*. London: Routledge.
Rosenholtz, S. (1989) *Teachers' Workplace: The Social Organisation of Schools*. London: Longman.
Russell, P. (1997) *The New Unitary Authorities: Inter-agency Collaboration*. SEN Policy Options seminar. Tamworth: NASEN.
Sammons, P., Thomas, S. and Mortimore, P. (1997) *Forging Links. Effective Schools and Effective Departments*. London: Paul Chapman.
SENCO-forum (1998) The SENCO-forum discussion on the Green Paper. http://www.mailbase.ac.uk/lists/senco-forum/files/welcome.html
Simkins, T. (1994) Efficiency, effectiveness and the local management of schools. *Journal of Education Policy*, 9 (1): 15–33.
Skrtic, T. (1991) Students with special educational needs: artifacts of the traditional curriculum, in M. Ainscow (ed.) *Effective Schools for All*. London: David Fulton.
Slavin, R. E. (1987) A theory of school and classroom organisation. *Educational Psychologist*, 22 (2): 98–108.

Sutcliffe, J. (1997) Danger: schools on the brink of overheating. *Times Educational Supplement*, 12 September.
TES (1997) Special needs then and now, *Times Educational Supplement*, 24 October: 8.
Thomas, G. (1997) Inclusive schools for an inclusive society. *British Journal of Special Education*, 24 (3): 103–7.
Thomas, G., Walker, D. and Webb, J. (1997) *The Making of the Inclusive School*. London: Routledge.
Thompson, G., Frances, J., Levačić, R. and Mitchell, J. (1991) *Markets, Hierarchies and Networks: The Coordination of Social Life*. London: Sage.
Tomlinson, J. (1994) The case for an intermediate tier, in S. Ranson and J. Tomlinson (eds) *School Co-operation: New Forms of Local Governance*. Harlow: Longman.
Touche Ross Management Consultants (1990) *Extending Local Management of Schools to Special Schools*. London: Touche Ross.
UNESCO (1994) *The Salamanca Statement and Framework for Action on Special Needs Education*. Paris: UNESCO.
Vevers, P. (1992) Getting in on the Act. *British Journal of Special Education*, 19 (3): 88–91.
Wedell, K. (1990) The 1988 Act and current principles of special educational needs, in H. Daniels and J. Ware (eds) *Special Educational Needs and the National Curriculum*. London: Kogan Page.
Wedell, K. (1995) Making inclusive education ordinary. *British Journal of Special Education*, 22 (3): 100–4.
Wedell, K. (1996) Education legislation 1988 to 1994, in M. Mittler and V. Sinason (eds) *Changing Policy and Practice for People with Learning Disabilities*. London: Cassell.
Wedell, K. (1997) The national curriculum, educational standards and the local management of schools, in *Implementing Inclusive Education*. Paris: OECD.
Wedell, K., Stevens, C., Waller, T. and Matheson, L. (1997) SENCOs sharing questions and solutions. *British Journal of Special Education*, 24 (4): 167–70.
West, A., David, M., Hailes, J. and Ribbens, J. (1995) The process of choosing secondary schools. *Educational Management and Administration*, 23 (1): 28–38.
Weston, P. and Barrett, E. with Jamison, J. (1992) *The Quest for Coherence*. Slough: NFER.
Whitty, G., Power, S. and Halpin, D. (1998) *Devolution and Choice in Education: The School, the State and the Market*. Buckingham: Open University Press.
Wolfendale, S. (1992) *Empowering Parents and Teachers – Working for Children*. London: Cassell.
Wright, J. and Graham, J. (1997) Speech and language therapists working with teachers. *British Journal of Special Education*, 24 (4): 171–4.
Wylie, T. (1997) Personal communication.

INDEX

accountability
  of cluster groups, 44, 74
  and resources, 76, 79
  of schools, 7
  and sharing expertise, 107
age-weighted pupil units (AWPU), 77
agencies, and the educational framework, 16
Ainscow, M., 123
Australia, 65
autonomy, of cluster groups, 69, 70

'back to basics', 89
Barber, M., 130
behaviour management in classes, 95
Behaviour Support Plans, 19, 109, 126
behavioural problems, 5, 9–10, 19, 113, 124
benefits
  of collaboration, 68, 73–4, 74–5
  for teachers, 101–3
  of shared resourcing, 86
Black Horse cluster, 48, 54–6, 61, 62, 68, 112
Blair, Tony, 124
Blunkett, David, 88, 126

'bottom-up' initiatives, in inter-agency collaboration, 118
'bottom-up' (school-led) cluster groups, 27, 42–3, 46, 69, 129
  and shared resourcing, 86
bureaucratic systems, 65, 66, 67

Children's Service Plans (CSPs), 109, 117, 125–6, 127, 129
civic society, development of a, 126, 127, 128, 131, 132
class, and parental choice of schools, 7, 11–12
classroom assistants, 56, 62, 111
cluster groups
  accountability, 74
  benefits of, 68, 73–4, 101–4
  Black Horse, 48, 54–6, 61, 62, 68, 112
  catalysing, 42, 43
  collaborative activities, 30–5, 45–65
  defining a cluster, 45–6
  extent of clustering, 40–1
  fitness for purpose, 41–2
  funding and resources, 33, 35, 36–7, 46, 68
    delegating to the group, 80–2
    and LEAs, 70, 71, 72
    sharing for SEN, 72–3

Index

Green Paper on proposals for, 21
high- and low-collaborating, 38–9
incentives for schools to collaborate, 70–1
management, 37–8, 63, 69–70
nature of clustering, 39–40
and networks, 46, 67–8
prevalence of, 26–7
purposes, 34–5
setting up, 69–70
sharing expertise with outside agencies, 107–8, 123
size and composition, 28–9, 38
and special needs provision, 30–5, 43
and specialist education services, 111–13
survey of, 25–44
The Valley, 47, 48–51, 69–70, 98
'top-down' or 'bottom-up', 27, 42–4, 46, 69, 129
and shared resourcing, 86
and sharing expertise, 113, 114
Wattford, 47, 51–4, 61, 62, 63
Weston, 48, 56–9, 61, 96
Woodside, 48, 59–60, 69, 113
Code of Practice, 5, 17
as a bureaucratic system, 66
and cluster groups, 42, 62
and effective learning, 92
and SENCOs (Special Educational Needs Coordinators), 96, 97, 98
Valley cluster, 50, 51
Weston cluster, 58, 59
and sharing expertise with outside agencies, 105–6, 107
and special educational needs, 18, 19
resources, 79
collaborative teaching, 99
communitarianism, 122, 129
community-based integrated programmes, 117–18
competition between schools
avoiding, 93
and cluster groups, 71
and collaboration activities, 61, 63
and special needs pupils, 121
and standards, 3
computer-assisted learning, 99
connexity, 122, 129
curriculum
comprehensive view of, 92
development, 22
see also National Curriculum

democratic control, and cluster groups, 44
Dessent, T., 115–16
DfE (Department for Education)
Choice and Diversity (White Paper), 10
defining special educational needs, 8–10
Education Bill (1998), 71
Excellence for All Children, see Green Paper
Excellence in Schools, see White Paper
disabled pupils
additional resourcing for, 85
in mainstream schools, 121

'Early Years Forum', 20
Early Years Partnership Development Plans, 109, 117, 126
economy of scale, and collaboration, 126–7
Education Action Zones, 20, 43, 126, 131

education services, sharing expertise within, 109, 110–14
education welfare officers, 10, 106
educational psychologists (EPs), see psychological service
educational reforms (1980s and 1990s), 7–8, 16–17
  and children with special educational needs, 13–16, 121–3
effectiveness, 3, 88, 119
  and collaboration, 19–23, 75, 123–6, 130
  and resource allocation, 79
efficiency, and resource allocation, 79
electronic communication, sharing expertise by, 116
emotional and behavioural difficulties, 9–10, 13, 19, 113, 124
employment prospects, and school achievement, 1
equity
  and markets in education, 66
  and resources, 22–3, 79
European Union, on strategies to reduce social exclusion, 124–5
examination results
  improving standards, 125
  league tables, 15, 23, 121
Excellence for All Children, see Green Paper
'exceptional need', and group resources, 81
exceptionality, 87
exclusions, see school exclusions

failing schools, 14, 18
'family of schools', Wattford cluster, 47, 51–4
federations, and clusters, 46

Fish Committee Report, 108, 114–15, 123
'foundation' schools, 17
funding
  collaboration and economy of scale, 126–7
  per capita, 10, 17
  for SEN pupils, 18
    Black Horse cluster, 55
    through individual statements, 19
    Weston cluster, 57–8
    Woodside cluster, 60
  see also resources

GCSE results, league tables for, 15, 23
GM (grant-maintained) schools, 9, 12–13, 15, 16–17, 22
governing bodies in schools, 13, 17
  and accountability, 74
  Black Horse cluster, 54
  and cluster groups, 43, 46, 70
Green Paper (on special educational needs), 4–5, 9, 10, 18, 20–1, 72, 75, 79, 80, 89, 109, 125
  and educational effectiveness, 124
  and inclusive education, 120–1
  and local government reorganization, 127
  and special schools, 113, 131
  and structures to facilitate cooperation, 122–3

headteachers
  Black Horse cluster, 55
  and cluster groups, 37, 42, 46
  benefits of, 73
  and federations, 46
  leadership of, 101
  Valley cluster, 49
  Wattford cluster, 51, 52, 53
  Weston cluster, 58

health services
  and cluster groups, 35
  collaboration with, 125–6
  sharing expertise with, 106, 109, 123
hearing impaired children, 111
hospital schools, 59, 60

inclusive communities, 126
inclusive education, 5, 88, 90–2, 119, 120–3
independent schools, 15
Individual Education Plans (IEPs), 40, 97
individual pupils
  holistic view of, 108–9
  resources for, 47, 77, 79, 86–7
individual schools
  and cluster groups, 33, 34, 36, 41
    incentives to collaborate, 70–1
  and collaborative groups of schools, 68
  and diversity of pupils' needs, 2
  implications of collaboration, 130–1
  resources, 36
  special educational needs policies, 94
    resourcing, 81
  'stuck' and 'moving', 92–3
INSET (in-service training)
  and the Black Horse cluster, 54, 55, 56
  by SENCOs, 103
  group resources for, 81, 83, 84
  and professional development, 95–6
  sharing expertise, 112–13
  survey of collaborative activities, 30, 31
  and the Valley cluster, 50
  and the Wattford cluster, 53

Labour Government
  and the educational framework, 11, 16–17, 21–2
  new policy climate, 129–30
  and SEN provision, 17–19, 119, 120–1
  and standards, 16, 18, 75, 119
language therapists, collaboration with teachers, 115
league tables, 11, 15, 21, 23, 77, 121
'learning society', 15
learning support assistants (LSAs), 83, 94, 98, 100, 105
learning support services, 110, 112
LEAs (local education authorities)
  Behaviour Support Plans, 19, 109, 126
  and the Black Horse cluster, 54, 56
  and cluster groups, 26–7, 36, 37–8, 40, 41, 42–3, 44, 61–2
    relative responsibilities, 71–2
    resourcing, 70, 71, 72
    supporting, 70, 71
  and collaboration, 20, 128–9
  development plans for coordination, 118
  DfE Green Paper on proposals for collaboration, 21
  Early Years Partnership Development Plans, 109, 117, 126
  and educational reforms, 7
  and high-collaborating cluster groups, 38–9
Literacy Strategies, 126

and the present educational
  framework, 17
resources
  cluster groups, 70, 71, 72,
    80–2
  SEN, 78–9, 80–2, 83
  and school funding, 10
  and sharing expertise with
    outside agencies, 106,
    110–13, 122–3
  and special education policies
    and practices, 9
  statement numbers maintained
    by, 89
  and the Valley cluster, 49–50
  and the Weston cluster group,
    57–8, 59
Lee, T., 22
legislation
  Children Act (1989), 109
  competition promoted through,
    93
  Education Act (1981), 80
  Education Act (1993), 12, 66
  Education Act (1997), 19
  Education Reform Act (1988),
    27, 47, 66
  and resources, 76–7, 78
Literacy Strategies, 126
LMS (local management of
  schools), 9, 16, 19, 46,
  128
  and SEN resources, 77, 80
  in the Valley cluster, 49
local communities
  and service coordination, 109,
    116–17
  and special schools, 122
local government
  models of, 128
  regional authorities, 43–4, 127,
    128
  reorganization, 127, 128
LSAs, *see* learning support
  assistants

mainstream schools
  additionally resourced, 85
  collaboration with special
    schools, 21, 28, 113–14
  and inclusive education, 121
  offering specialist services,
    43
  and sharing resources, 86–7
  and special needs pupils, 3, 5,
    9, 18, 123–4
Mallett, B., 105
management
  of cluster groups, 37–8
  of schools, 89
'market' approach to education,
  10–13, 15, 20, 21, 65–6,
  119
Moss, P., 126, 131
'moving' schools, 92–3
Mulgan, G., 130

National Curriculum, 3, 16, 46,
  77, 92
  Level 4 targets, 89
  review, 125
National Literacy Strategy, 89
Netherlands, 2–3
networks, 66–8
  and clusters, 46, 67–8
New Zealand, 65

OECD (Centre for Educational
  Research and Innovation),
  88, 108, 109, 117–18
Ofsted inspection reports, 11–12,
  16, 19, 74
  on SENCOs (Special
    Educational Needs
    Coordinators), 96–7
  and staffing of services, 108
open enrolment, 10, 17, 19

parent support, 99
parental choice of schools, 7,
  11–12, 121

avoiding competition between schools, 93
and children with special educational needs, 13–14
and cluster groups, 61
commitment to, 80
and the Wattford cluster, 53
parents
of children with special needs, 5, 11, 66
benefits of collaboration for, 103–4
and cluster groups, 70
and community-based integrated programmes, 118
and equity of resources, 23
and group SENCOs, 99
and inclusive education, 5
and networks, 67
and non-educational service provision, 116–17
sharing of expertise with school staff, 105–6
peer tutoring, 99
Petrie, P., 126, 131
physically impaired children, 114, 127
physiotherapists, collaboration with teachers, 115
pre-school children, 'Early Years Forum', 20
preventative work, 108
primary schools
developing special needs policies, 101
exclusions from, 19
funds for pupils with moderate learning difficulties, 82
and non-education service provision, 117
SENCOs in, 97
professional development, 94–6, 129
school and group SENCOs, 99–100

psychological service, 32, 47, 84
sharing expertise, 106, 110, 111, 112
Valley cluster, 50
Wattford cluster, 52
Weston cluster, 59
Pugach, M.C., 91
pupil diversity, 2, 3, 5
pupils
benefits of collaboration for, 102–3
excluded from schools, 5, 9–10, 14, 19, 75, 121, 124
failing, 88

quangos, 16, 43
quasi-market in education, 7, 10, 17, 65, 121

Ranson, S., 14, 15–16
regional authorities, 43–4, 127, 128
resource centres
benefits for teachers, 103
Black Horse cluster, 55–6, 112
and staff development, 96
Weston cluster, 58
resources, 2
Black Horse cluster, 54, 55
cluster groups, 62–3, 68
and LEAs, 70, 71, 72
shared use of, 72–3, 84–5
survey of, 33, 35, 36–7
and cost-effectiveness, 131–2
and equity, 22–3
and individual pupils, 47, 77
problem of 'resource drift', 77
resource paradox, 79
SEN, 76–87, 131
additional resourcing to a school in the group, 85
and competition between schools, 121–2
delegating to the group of schools, 80–2

and economy of scale, 126–7
for individual pupils, 47, 77, 79, 86–7
and joint appointments to a group of schools, 83–4
matched-funding for collaboration, 82–3
sharing, 72–3, 84–7, 96
targeting to schools most in need, 86
Valley cluster, 49–50
Wattford cluster, 52
Weston cluster group, 57–8
see also funding
Ridings School, Halifax, 14
rights of children and young people, 3–4
rural schools
and 'meaningful' groupings, 116
shared use of resources, 84
Valley cluster, 47, 48–51, 69–70
Wattford cluster, 51
Russell, P., 125–6

Salamanca World Statement on Special Needs Education, 4, 120
school exclusions, 5, 9–10, 14, 19, 75, 121, 124
school improvement, 88
secondary schools, and non-education service provision, 117
SEN support services, 32, 33
and resources, 77, 83
sharing expertise, 106, 111–13
in the Wattford cluster, 52, 53
see also special educational needs
SENCOs (Special Educational Needs Coordinators)
benefits of cluster groups, 73–4
and cluster group management, 69
collaboration between, in groupings of schools, 96–7
collaboration with teachers, 102–3
and effective learning, 92
and external agencies, 116
and group resources, 81
for a group of schools, 22, 48, 83, 98–100, 103
networks of, 131
and SEN resourcing, 80
sharing expertise, 105–6, 108, 110
and specialist education services, 111, 112
in survey of cluster groups, 32, 33, 35, 37, 40, 46
Valley cluster, 50–1
Wattford cluster, 51, 52–3, 54
Weston cluster, 48, 58–9
Woodside cluster, 60
shared resources, 72–3, 84–7, 96
Slavin, R.E., 90–1
small schools, 22
and SNASTs (special needs advisory support teachers), 84
Valley cluster, 48–51, 69–70
SNASTs (special needs advisory support teachers), 84
social deprivation
and community-based integrated programmes, 118
and 'Education Action Zones', 20
and failing schools, 18
and school achievement, 1, 88–9
and special needs pupils, 9, 14, 48
Social Exclusion Unit, 124

Index

social services
  and cluster groups, 35
  sharing expertise with, 106, 109, 122
special educational needs (SEN), 1–2, 3–5
  and cluster groups, 30–5, 43, 74–5
    collaboration in action, 45–64
    sharing resources, 72–3
  current provisions, 17–19, 119
  defining, 8–10
  and educational reforms, 7–8, 13–16
  and inclusive education, 90–2
  policies of schools, 94
  resources, 72–3, 76–87, 96
  Salamanca World Statement on, 4, 120
  sharing expertise with outside agencies, 105–18
  Tribunal, 78
  see also Green Paper; SENCOs; statements
special needs service managers, 111
special schools
  allocating resources to, 80
  in the Black Horse cluster, 54
  as centres of excellence, 28, 43
  collaboration with mainstream schools, 21, 28, 113–14, 123
  proportion of children in, 9, 18
  as resource bases for local schools, 122, 131
  standards of, 18
  in survey of cluster groups, 28, 29, 35, 36, 37
  Weston cluster group, 48, 56–7
speech therapists, collaboration with teachers, 115
'stakeholder society', 122, 129

standards, 1
  and competition between schools, 3
  and cost-effectiveness, 132
  and educational reforms, 7, 10
  and government policy, 16, 18, 75, 119
  LEA monitoring of, 71
  raising, 88–9
  and special educational needs, 18–19
statements (of special educational needs)
  and the benefits of collaboration, 104
  as a bureaucratic system, 66
  and funding, 19
  and parental choice of school, 12
  proportions of children given, 17
  reducing number of, 72–3, 75, 79, 87
  rising numbers of, 76, 77–8, 89
  school levels of response to, 90
  and special/mainstream school collaboration, 113–14
  Wattford cluster group, 47
  see also individual pupils
'stuck' schools, 92–3

teachers
  benefits of collaboration for, 101–3
  Black Horse cluster, 54, 55, 56
  collaboration with non-education services, 115
  collaboration with SENCOs, 102–3
  and cross-cluster training, 62
  and educational effectiveness, 123
  as governors in schools, 54
  joint appointments of SEN staff, 97–100

meeting diverse needs of pupils, 2
professional development, 94–6, 99–100, 129
and schools' special educational needs policies, 94
sharing expertise, 105–6, 107, 108
SNASTs (special needs advisory support teachers), 84
special needs advisory, 55, 56, 111, 112
and special/mainstream school collaboration, 113–14
studies of teacher support schemes, 130
Weston cluster, 58
and whole-class teaching, 90–1
see also headteachers; SENCOs (Special Educational Needs Coordinators)
testing pupils, league tables of results, 11
'top-down' initiatives, in inter-agency collaboration, 118
'top-down' (LEA-led) cluster groups, 27, 42–4, 46, 69, 129
and shared resourcing, 86
and sharing expertise, 113, 114

transition (from primary to secondary school)
collaboration activities, 61, 63
and group SENCOs, 98
and networks, 67

United States of America, 65

Valley cluster, 47, 48–51, 69–70, 96, 98
'value-added' test results, 11, 23, 121
visually impaired children, 111, 127
voluntary services, sharing expertise with, 106

Warnock Report (1978), 78, 113
Wattford cluster, 47, 51–4, 61, 62, 63
Wedell, K., 91
Weston cluster, 48, 56–9, 61, 96
White Paper (*Excellence in Schools*), 16, 19, 20, 21, 88, 119, 122
whole-class teaching, 89, 90–1
Wolfendale, S., 105–6
Woodside cluster, 48, 59–60, 61–2, 69, 113

Youth Service Plans, 117

MANAGING SPECIAL EDUCATION
CODES, CHARTERS AND COMPETITION

John Fish and Jennifer Evans

How can the educational and other special needs of children and young people with disabilities and/or significant learning difficulties be met by policies which emphasize competition, market forces and short-term financial planning?

This is the key issue which concerns *Managing Special Education*. The book discusses a number of persistent and unresolved issues about the relationship of special education to primary, secondary and further education.

Local management of schools and colleges and increased parental choice have created new and difficult market conditions for special educational provision. Increased choice costs money and the more special the need, the greater the cost. How will responsibilities delegated to schools and colleges ensure that children, young people and adults with disabilities and learning difficulties have reasonable access to quality educational opportunities, given that the market system provides no incentives for schools and colleges to provide higher cost minority provision unless it is self-financing?

This book is both topical and forward looking. It concludes with a possible agenda for the future which identifies both issues to be resolved and management tasks from central government to schools and colleges.

Contents
Education and individual differences – The new framework – Perspectives in 1993 – Basic issues and policy development – Meeting needs in Schools – A range of provision – Post-16 further and continuing education – Funding special education – Major themes revisited – An agenda for the future – Bibliography – Index.

144pp   0 335 19438 9 (Paperback)   0 335 19439 7 (Hardback)

STRUGGLES FOR INCLUSIVE EDUCATION
AN ETHNOGRAPHIC STUDY
Anastasia D. Vlachou

> This is a lucid, authoritative and original study of teachers' views and attitudes towards the integration into mainstream schooling of a particular group of children defined as having special educational needs. It offers one of the clearest and most comprehensive analyses of the socio-political mechanisms by which the 'special' are socially constructed and excluded from the normal education system that has so far been produced.
>
> Sally Tomlinson,
> Professor of Educational Policy at Goldsmiths College,
> University of London

In its detailed analysis of primary school teachers' and pupils' attitudes towards integration, this book locates the question of inclusive education within the wider educational context. The wealth of original interview material sheds new light on the reality of everyday life in an educational setting, and shows us the nature and intensity of the struggles experienced by both teachers and pupils in their efforts to promote more inclusive school practices. The author's sensitive investigation of the relationship between teachers' contradictory views of the 'special' and their integration, and the wider social structures in which teachers work, adds to our understanding of the inevitable difficulties in promoting inclusive educational practices within a system which functions via exclusive mechanisms.

The book will be of interest to students of education, sociology and disability as well as teachers and policy-makers involved in inclusive education. The original methodologies adopted when working with children will also appeal to students of attitudinal, disability and educational research.

Contents
Introduction – Part 1: Setting the theoretical scene – Disability, normality and special needs – Towards a better understanding of attitudes – Part 2: Teachers' perspectives – Teachers and the changing culture of teaching – Teachers' attitudes towards integration (with reference to pupils with Down's Syndrome) – Part 3: Children's perspectives – Integration: the children's point of view – Disabled children and children's culture – Conclusion – Appendix 1: The problem of ethical integrity – Appendix 2: Participants in the study – Appendix 3: The role of the photograph in interviews with children – References – Index.

208pp   0 335 19763 9 (Paperback)   0 335 19764 7 (Hardback)